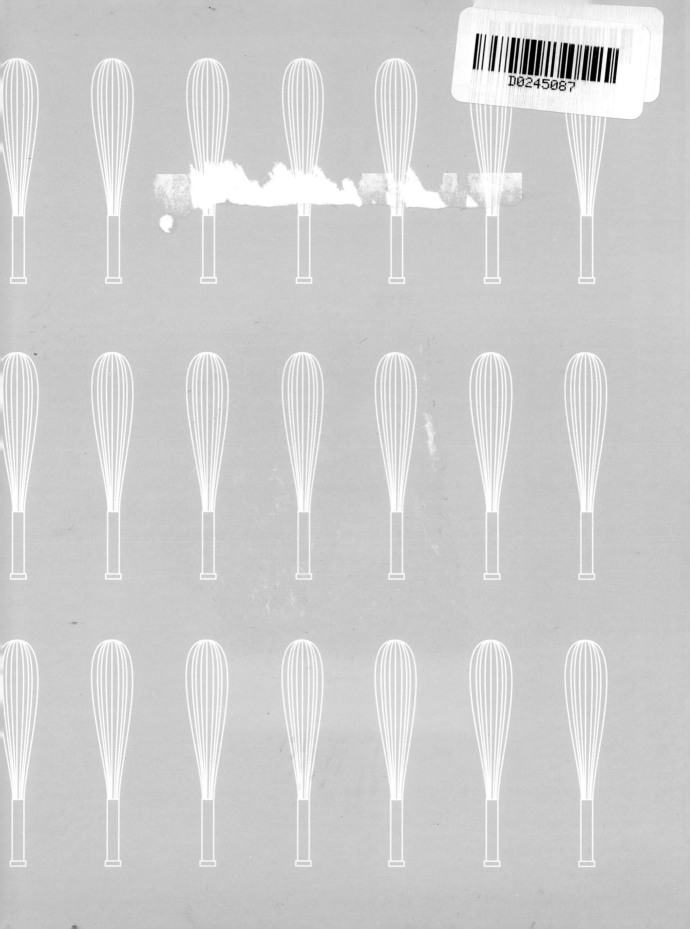

Good Housekeeping

THE BOOK OF
CAKE
DECORATING

Good Housekeeping

THE BOOK OF
CAKE
DECORATING

Meike Beck

Cookery Editor, Good Housekeeping

COLLINS & BROWN

First published in Great Britain in 2012
by Collins & Brown
10 Southcombe Street
London W14 0RA

An imprint of Anova Books Company Ltd

The Good Housekeeping website is
www.allaboutyou.com/goodhousekeeping

ISBN 978-190844-900-9

A catalogue record for this book is available from the
British Library.

Reproduction by Dot Gradations Ltd, UK
Printed and bound by 1010 Printing International Ltd, China

This book can be ordered direct from the publisher.
Contact the marketing department, but try your
bookshop first.

www.anovabooks.com

NOTES

Both metric and imperial measures are given for the
recipes. Follow either set of measures, not a mixture of
both, as they are not interchangeable.

All spoon measures are level.
1 tsp = 5ml spoon; 1 tbsp = 15ml spoon.

Ovens and grills must be preheated to the specified
temperature.

Medium eggs should be used except where otherwise
specified. Free-range eggs are recommended.

Note that some recipes contain raw or lightly cooked eggs.
The young, elderly, pregnant women and anyone with an
immune-deficiency disease should avoid these because of
the slight risk of salmonella.

Photographers: Martin Brigdale (page 107); Nicki Dowey
(pages 25, 78T, 104, 105, 113, 128, 130, 131, 134, 148 and 151);
Emma Lee (page 103); William Lingwood (pages 2, 6, 13, 15,
17, 23, 24R, 32, 35, 38L, 39B, 42, 51, 52, 53, 54, 55, 56, 61, 63B,
64, 65, 66, 67, 68, 70, 71B, 75, 76, 77, 79, 80, 82, 83, 84, 85,
86, 92, 112, 115, 116, 133, 137, 138, 140, 142, 144, 147 and 171);
Gareth Morgans (page 109); Myles New (pages 98 and 119);
Craig Robertson (pages 22, 39T, 93T, 93B, 94L, 94M, 94R,
96B, 95, 96T and 97); Lucinda Symons (pages 31, 33, 34, 36,
58, 59, 62, 63T, 101, 120, 123, 150, 153, 154, 155, 156, 157, 158,
159, 160, 161, 162, 163, 164, 165, 166, 167, 168, 16 and 170);
Martin Thompson (page 30); Philip Web (pages 106 and
110); Kate Whitaker (page 111)

Home Economists: Joanna Farrow, Emma Jane Frost,
Teresa Goldfinch, Alice Hart, Lucy McKelvie, Kim Morphew,
Aya Nishimura, Bridget Sargeson and Mari Mererid Williams

Stylists: Tamzin Fernando, Wei Tang, Helen Trent and
Fanny Ward

Icing Techniques: Cakes4Fun, London (page 61)

Cover photograph: Myles New

Contents

6   Foreword

8   **Planning for the Occasion**

18   **Cake Basics**

40   **Icing, Frosting & Covering Cakes**

72   **Cake Decorating**

88   **Chocolate & Sugar**

98   **Special Occasion Cakes**

126   **Novelty Cakes**

148   **Cupcakes**

172   Glossary
174   Index

Foreword

One of my very favourite pastimes is whiling away hours in specialised cake decorating shops. The tiny plunge cutters, leaf impression moulds, trinket jars of edible powders, bottles of colourful pastes and boxes of paint brushes and odd-shaped plastic tools have such a pull on me that I think my hobby could easily slip into an full-blown obsession. I even have dedicated floor-to-ceiling storage in my home that has been affectionately christened 'my cake cupboard', much to my husband's eternal bemusement.

Luckily, I know I'm not alone in my chosen pastime and that cake baking and decorating are ever increasing in popularity. We receive hundreds of emails and letters a month from dedicated readers, seeking advice on how to create their dream cake. Wonderful news, and we're always happy to help!

Thankfully the world of cake decorating has changed remarkably in recent years, insomuch as sugar crafting used to be the occupation and hobby of only the majestically talented and patient. Every single petal and leaf sprig had to be moulded by hand with materials that were tempestuous to say the least – hence many flower sprays were varnished and kept in display cabinets. They were works of art that mere mortals could never hope to replicate … but now, with well-advised know-how and many more tools at our disposal, anything is possible.

Unfortunately, there's an unfounded fear of baking that exists among the uninitiated, but all it takes is the sight of a cooling cake resting on a wire rack, or the pride you feel when a cake is fully decorated to banish this fear completely. Then you'll really know you've caught the baking bug … and there's no looking back.

Filled with detailed description, helpful step-by-step instructions, endless pictures and many triple-tested recipes, this book is all you need to create masterful cakes in the comfort of your own kitchen.

I very much hope you make use of this book; it contains the potential for endless joy.

Meike.

Cookery Editor
Good Housekeeping

Planning for the Occasion

When you're making any type of celebration cake, it is really important to think through and plan every single detail of the cake carefully. So often it is easy to rush into making the cake with little thought of who the cake is for, the type of mixture to be used, the shape, size or even decoration. The occasion for which the cake is being made often dictates the type of cake you are making, whether it is a wedding cake, christening, anniversary, novelty or birthday cake.

Things to take into consideration when planning a celebration cake

- Your skill level – if you are inexperienced, try not to be overly ambitious. Let your skills influence the design, as the finished cake must be beautiful.
- For whom the cake is being made – ask them if they have any preferences. If the event is not obvious (like a wedding or a christening), then the person may have a particular interest, skill or hobby that the finished cake can relate to.
- The type of occasion for which the cake is being made, whether formal or informal.
- The shape and size of the cake, bearing in mind how many guests there will be.

- The design and the time available to complete the cake. If time is short, obviously a simple cake well finished is better than an intricate cake that might have to be rushed.
- Does the chosen cake mixture fit the event, i.e. can it be stored once baked or does it need to be eaten immediately. A fruit cake, for example, can be made months in advance whereas a sponge cake is more last-minute.
- The colour scheme and type of icing required. If possible, acquire fabric samples or swatches, thread, flowers or ribbons, so that you have a guide.
- Transportation of the finished cake whether it needs any last-minute assembly (in which case pack your tools!).

On top of the initial planning, there are also other factors to take into account. Do you have the correct cake tins? There are so many nowadays to choose from: hexagonal, octagonal, round, square, oval, petal, heart-shaped, horseshoe and endless novelty variations, to name but a few. The advantage of these tin shapes is that they give more scope for unusual designs to fit certain occasions. Many are sold in specialist cake shops and via websites; alternatively, cake tins can often be hired from specialist cake shops for a charge or hire fee.

Designing a cake

Cake designing is the most important aspect of cake decorating. Once the shape and size of the cake has been decided, this gives you a base on which to plan your design.

- The base colour of the cake will have a strong impact on the finished design. White or ivory are the most traditional choices for classic celebration cakes.
- There are two main icing choices for formal cakes – the clean, sharp, classical lines of royal icing, or the rounded, smooth finish of sugarpaste (also known as fondant).

These two very different mediums dramatically change the overall appearance of the cake and also the choice of decoration.
- Let yourself be inspired by fabric and wallpaper books, china, ceramic or embroidery patterns.

Time plan for making a cake

When you have committed to making a celebration or novelty cake, quite some time can be spent worrying about when to complete certain stages. It is always best to work backwards from the date the cake is required and draw up a time plan (remember to allow drying time for marzipan and different icings, as well as for making any decorations). When you know exactly on which day to complete certain tasks, the project becomes more manageable. Remember to look at your recipe for an idea of how long each stage will take, as well as storage guidelines.

Here is a rough time plan for making a celebration fruit cake

2–3 months before
Make the cake. When it is cold, prick the top of the cake at intervals with a fine skewer and spoon some brandy (1–2 tbsp) evenly over the surface. Wrap the cooled cake in a double layer of greaseproof paper and then in a double thickness of foil. Store for at least 1 month, but preferably 2–3 months, in a cool, dry place. Feed every few weeks with brandy as above (no need to prick additional holes), and wrap as before.

3–4 weeks before
The baked cake should have an even top, but if not it can be levelled with a sharp knife. Apply the apricot glaze and almond paste or marzipan to the cake (see page 49–50), cover loosely and store in a cool dry place for one to two weeks before applying the icing.

10–14 days before
If using royal icing, apply the first layer (see page 43), and leave to dry for the recommended time. Consolidate the design of the cake, and check you have your ribbons, pearl-topped pins, cake board, pillars, dowels, and so on.

8–12 days before
If using royal icing, apply the second coat if necessary and leave to dry. Start making any separate run-out, modelled or stamped decorations and leave to dry as instructed.

7 days before
Make sure any applied decorations are made at least two days before fixing them to the iced cake; preferably complete all decorating a week before the due date. If needed, practise piped designs on a board or upturned plate to avoid making mistakes on the cake. If using pillars or dowels, make sure the positions are established and the materials are ready.

If your cake needs to be transported, finalise the details. Write a list of equipment you'll need to take with you for last-minute assembly.

5–7 days before
If covering the cake with sugarpaste, do so now and leave it to harden.

1–2 days before
Assemble the cake either at home or at the location.

After the celebration
Wrap any leftover cake in greaseproof paper and then in a double thickness of foil. Store for up to two months in a cool dry place. If you plan on storing the cake for longer, then wrap as above and freeze until needed. Many will recommend freezing a cake for only six months, but wrapped and frozen in this way the cake should keep well for years. To serve, thaw completely, then remove all the icing and almond paste or marzipan. Check the cake still looks and tastes good, then cover once again with fresh almond paste or marzipan and your choice of icing.

Cake sizes and cake boards

If making a tiered cake, consider the number of tiers you need and whether you want to stack them directly on top of one another or support each tier by pillars. Stack the empty cake tins (base facing upwards) on top of each other to give you a helpful visual to work from. As a rough guide, when deciding on the sizes for a tiered cake, allow 5–7.5cm (2–3 inches) between the tin sizes if your final cake is going to have pillars separating the cakes. If stacking the cakes on top of each other, the cakes need to have a 7.5–10cm (3–4 inches) difference in size. Good proportions for an average three-tier cake are 30.5cm (12 inches), 23cm (9 inches) and 15cm (6 inches).

Cake boards also play an important part in the cake design and overall appearance. In general, cake boards need to be 5–7.5cm (2–3 inches) larger than the cake to allow for the addition of the marzipan, icing and decoration, but the design of the cake must also be considered when selecting cake boards. Remember, if the finished cake includes run-out collars, extension work or sugar pieces, allow extra width on the cake board to prevent any damage to the decoration. If in any doubt about the size, allow more rather than less. If you do not like the look of a silver, gold or coloured cake board, it can always be covered very satisfactorily with your chosen colour of icing (see page 54).

How much mixture to bake shaped cakes?

If you want to make a shaped cake, such as a number or a heart, there's a simple way to calculate how much mixture you will need to fill a tin. For every 600ml (1 pint) of water the tin will hold, you will need mixture made with the ingredients listed below, so multiply up as required. Remember to fill the tin only as deep as you want the finished cake to be – not necessarily to the very top.

Victoria sandwich cake mixture – giving 600ml (1 pint)

50g (2oz) unsalted butter or margarine

50g (2oz) caster sugar

1 medium egg

50g (2oz) self-raising flour

1 **Make the Victoria sandwich** in the usual way (see page 30), then bake in an oven preheated to 190°C (170°C fan oven) mark 5. The baking time will vary according to the shape and depth of the cake.

2 To test whether the cake is ready, gently press the centre of the sponge, it should feel springy. Alternatively, insert a skewer into the centre of the cake – it should come out clean. Once baked, leave the cake to cool for 5 minutes in the tin, then turn out on to a wire rack and leave to cool completely.

Fruit cake mixture – giving 600ml (1 pint)

75g (3oz) unsalted butter or margarine

75g (3oz) soft brown sugar

1½ medium eggs

100g (3½oz) plain flour

¼ tsp mixed spiced

175g (6oz) currants

50g (2oz) sultanas

50g (2oz) raisins

12 glacé cherries, halved

50g (2oz) chopped mixed peel

1 **For the Fruit Cake**, line your chosen cake tin (see page 22) and preheat the oven to 150°C (130°C fan) mark 2. In a large bowl, cream together the butter or margarine and sugar until fluffy. Gradually add the eggs, beating well after each addition.

2 Sift the flour and mixed spice into the butter bowl, then fold into the mixture with a large metal spoon. Add the remaining ingredients and fold to combine. Spoon into the cake tin and bake (the baking time will vary according to the size and depth of your cake).

3 To test whether the fruit cake is ready, insert a skewer into the centre of the cake – it should come out clean. If it doesn't, return the cake to the oven for 15 minutes and test again. Leave the fruit cake to cool completely in the tin before turning out.

Equipment

A selection of basic equipment is compulsory in order to bake and decorate cakes successfully. The comprehensive list of equipment overleaf highlights basic items needed to produce consistently good cakes, as well as specialist materials for producing more sophisticated results. Start with a few basic items and add to your collection as your skills increase (and as the demands of the recipe dictate). Remember that kitchen equipment is subject to a great deal of wear and tear, so look for good-quality items. Store and clean your equipment carefully following each use.

ELECTRICAL EQUIPMENT

❶ Food processors
Perfect for making pastry, breadcrumbs or for chopping large quantities of ingredients quickly. Also good for some types of cake mixes. Most come with a number of blade attachments – dough hooks, graters, slicers, and so on.

❷ Blenders and stick blenders
Less versatile than food processors, but useful for certain jobs, such as puréeing fruit. If you don't have space for an upright blender, then a stick blender is useful.

❸ Freestanding mixers
These powerful machines are particularly useful to speed up any mixing, whisking or kneading. Hugely versatile, but expensive and they take up a fair amount of space.

❹ Hand-held electric mixers
Invaluable for all types of cake making. They ensure a good volume and quick results. Particularly useful for creaming together butter and sugar or for making meringues. They don't take up a lot of space and can be packed away easily.

Electrical equipment

BASIC EQUIPMENT

◆1 Scales

Accurate measurement is essential when following most baking recipes. The electronic scale is the most accurate and usually weighs in increments of 1–5g. Buy one with a flat platform on which you can put your bowl or measuring jug. Always set the scale to zero before adding the ingredients and use either metric or imperial measurements, do not mix them.

◆2 Measuring jugs, ◆3 cups and ◆4 spoons

Jugs can be plastic, metal or glass and are available in various sizes marked with both metric and imperial measures. Measuring cups are classically used in American recipes and are usually bought as sets of ¼, ⅓, ½ and 1 cups. It is essential to use calibrated measuring spoons in all baking recipes. Do not be tempted to reach into the cutlery drawer since general spoons used in the kitchen may vary in size, which will affect the accuracy of the recipe. If you don't have any measuring spoons, then go by the rule that 1 tbsp is equal to 15ml, and 1 tsp is equal to 5ml. Measuring spoons can be plastic, ceramic or metal and often come in sets attached together.

◆5 Mixing bowls

A selection of small, medium and large bowls are essential for good cake making. Choose bowls in glass, plastic, china or stainless steel with smooth, rounded insides for thorough and even mixing.

Stainless steel bowls work best when you need to chill a mixture down quickly in the fridge or heat it up over simmering water (when melting chocolate, for example). Do not use stainless steel bowls in the microwave.

Plastic or glass bowls are best if you need to use them in the microwave.

◆6 Mixing spoons

For general mixing, the cheap and sturdy wooden spoon is best. The spoon should be stiff, so that it can cope with thick mixtures. In addition, a large metal spoon for folding items together is also invaluable.

◆7 Spatulas

Essential for scraping out all the mixture from mixing bowls. The best have a silicone head, which moulds easily to the bowl. Also useful for folding ingredients together.

◆8 Sieves

A variety of fine wire mesh or nylon sieves are always needed to strain out ingredients or aerate dry ingredients, such as flour, cocoa powder and icing sugar.

◆9 Wire whisk

A flexible wire whisk is necessary for whisking all types of mixtures to obtain volume and give smooth consistencies. Generally, the larger the whisk the more efficient it is.

◆10 Palette knife

For basic baking, a simple large straight-bladed palette knife will do most jobs. Ideal for loosening cakes from tins and spreading and smoothing icing.

◆11 Brushes

For general glazing, brushes are available in many sizes with bristle or silicone tips. Take care as bristle brushes can moult when they get old, or become stiff if not cleaned properly.

◆12 Rolling pin

Essential for even rolling of pastry, dough, sugarpaste, and so on. Rolling pins come in different lengths, thicknesses and materials. Wooden varieties are generally cheap and universally effective, whereas silicone pins are more costly but ideal if rolling lots of pastry or sugarpaste, as they give a more even appearance.

◆13 Ruler or ◆14 tape measure and ◆15 scissors

Accurate measurement during cake baking and decorating is essential to guarantee good results. Sharp kitchen scissors are frequently needed for cutting out cake tin lining papers, templates, florists wire, etc.

◆16 Vegetable peeler

Choose one that fits your hand comfortably, either swivel-headed or y-shaped, depending on your preference.

◆17 Graters

Either box or hand-held, graters are mostly used in baking for grating citrus zest or chocolate. Look for sturdy models that are comfortable to hold, as they will need to withstand pressure. Graters give coarse, medium-coarse or fine results.

◆18 Cake tins

The right cake tins are invaluable when it comes to baking all types of cakes. They vary tremendously in the quality and thickness of the metal, the finish, the sizing and the depth, so care must be taken when choosing them – try to buy the best quality you can afford. Tins may be single-piece, loose-bottomed or springform. Always measure the tin with a ruler across the base to ascertain its size. Never be temped to use a different shape or size of tin than the recipe states, otherwise the baking time, texture, depth and appearance of the cake will be affected.

19 Baking trays/baking sheets
These have many uses in baking
and either have a lipped edge or are
completely flat. Choose ones that are
large (but which fit comfortably in
your oven) to avoid having to bake in
batches. Buy the best you can afford
to avoid any warping when in contact
with heat.

20 Wire racks
Available in different sizes and shapes,
with wide or narrow mesh. Each has
its own use, so have a selection.

21 Knives
A selection of small, medium and
large knives with both straight and
serrated blades are needed for
preparing ingredients and cutting
cakes into layers.

22 Papers
There are a variety of papers, such
as greaseproof, non-stick baking
parchment, waxed paper, rice paper
and brown paper, which all have their
uses. Greaseproof paper, being all
purpose, is suitable for lining cake
tins. Non-stick baking parchment is
ideal for meringues, spreading melted
chocolate, drying moulded or cut-out
sugar decorations – in short, ensuring
nothing sticks. Waxed paper is fine
and flexible and is ideal for icing run-
outs and to trace over designs for
piped decorations. Rice paper is used
for biscuits and macaroons; it adheres
to the mixture, can be baked and is
edible. Brown paper is used to fit around
the outside of cake tins to protect the
cake during long periods of baking.

23 Other useful bakeware
Loaf tins, tart tins (fluted and plain),
sandwich tins, pie tins, muffin tins.
Reusable, non-stick, silicone baking
mats and liners, muffin trays and
cupcake moulds.

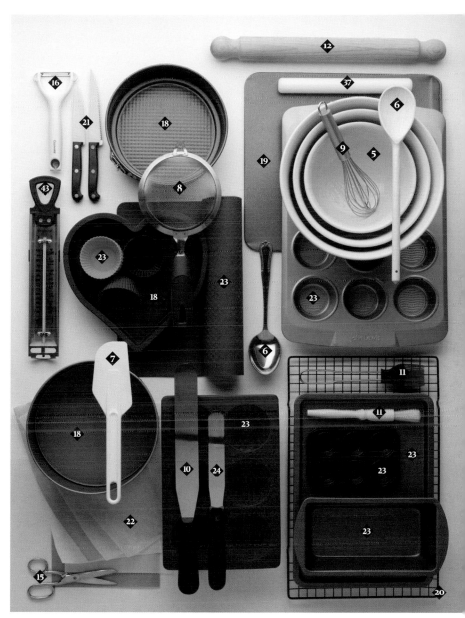

Bakeware equipment

SPECIALIST EQUIPMENT

24 Small palette knives
Small straight and crank-handled palette knives are ideal for lifting and transferring small and fragile icing decorations, spreading royal icing on to cakes and smoothing to the edges.

25 Piping bags
Indispensable for piping icings and meringues. The most convenient are the disposable ones – try to buy ones with added grip. Alternatively, use the nylon ones, but make sure you wash them thoroughly in hot soapy water after each use.

26 Piping pumps
Icing pumps are usually sold as part of an icing set, complete with nozzles. They are made of metal or polythene and consist of a large tube with screw nozzles at one end and a plunger at the other end. The plunger unscrews for easy refilling and the pump dismantles for hygienic cleaning.

The disadvantage of the icing pump is that you cannot 'feel' how the icing is reacting to the pressure applied to the plunger – this may result in too little or too much icing being pushed through the nozzle at the other end. Also, it is essential that the consistency of the icing is correct for good results.

27 Piping nozzles
Basic piping work can be achieved with just a few nozzles (check the recipe for the size of nozzle needed – often numerical). More sophisticated piping will require a large selection of piping nozzles, with varying tip sizes and shapes.

28 Cake boards
Available in many shapes, sizes and colours, cake boards give a professional finish to your cake. The larger the cake, the thicker and more substantial the board needs to be.

29 Cake smoothers
These help to smooth the surface of sugarpaste to obtain a satin-smooth finish and to eliminate any cracks or imperfections.

30 Sugarpaste modelling tools
Cutting knife, cone, bone and ball tools all have a purpose when working with sugarpaste, and for experimental cake decorators are well worth buying.

31 Sugarpaste mats
These non-stick mats often come with pre-marked circles and grids for accurate, mark-free rolling. Many textured mats are also available.

32 Fine brushes
Fine artist's brushes are available in many different shapes and sizes and are useful for painting with food colourings. Also useful when making run-outs.

33 Foam pads
Cheap to buy and essential for supporting sugar and flower-paste decorations and enabling them to dry in the correct shape.

34 Run-out film
This fine transparent plastic film can be used for making accurate run-out decorations, which slide easily off the film when they are dry. Can be tricky to source.

35 Scribing needle
Used for etching the surface of iced cakes in order to transfer designs from templates.

36 Crimpers
These tweezer-style tools have decorative end pieces that imprint various designs on the surface of sugarpaste.

37 Small acrylic rolling pin
Great for smoothly rolling out small quantities of icing and creating frills, petals and waves.

38 Craft knife
Ideal for cutting out shapes made from sugarpaste and for veining leaves.

39 Embossing stamps
Stamps that have raised designs of flowers, motifs, letters, or seasonal emblems. Used to transfer designs on to sugarpaste.

40 Florist's wire
Available in gauges from very fine to thick, usually coated in white, green or brown tape. Used in sugarcraft for wiring flowers or leaves into sprays.

41 Stamens
Usually sold in bundles, stamens make up the centre of non-edible sugarcraft flowers. A vast variety of colour, size and finish is available to suit all sugarcraft flowers.

42 Ribbon slotters and insertion blades
These tools are wonderful for making neat slits in the surface of sugarpaste, and helping inserting the ribbons.

43 Thermometer
An accurate sugar thermometer is needed for testing the temperature of sugar syrup when making some icings, as well as for tempering chocolate.

44 Turntable
Turntables comprise a heavy base and a flat top that rotates. There are many qualities to choose from. They

are essential for evenly turning a cake while icing and decorating to get good results.

45 Straight edge

This is a long, inflexible metal ruler that is used to obtain a smooth, flat finish on the surface of a royal iced cake. There are different lengths available, but a 30.5cm (12 inch) straight edge is easy to handle on cakes up to 25.5cm (10 inches).

46 Side scrapers

These are used to smooth royal icing on the side of cakes. They are made from plastic or stainless steel. They are also available patterned with ingrained patterns, to give a variety of designs to the sides of the cake.

47 Pillars and 48 dowels

Cake pillars (either hollow or solid) separate the layers of a tiered cake, but they don't always have to be used. Dowels, which are usually acrylic, are inserted into sugarpasted cakes to support the tiers, as the icing alone is not strong enough. They are hygienic and trimmed to the level of the cake.

Cutters (not shown)

A set of plain round and fluted metal cutters have many uses in cake decorating. Fancy flower, leaf, novelty or biscuit cutters are available in many shapes and sizes, and you'll find endless uses for them. Plunge cutters, which eject the sugarpaste shape by use of a spring plunger, are wonderfully easy to use and give professional results.

Icing nails (see page 65)

Icing nails look like small upturned saucers of metal or polythene mounted on a nail – like mini turntables. They are held in the hand, and used as a rotating surface when piping flowers. A little icing is spread on the surface of the nail and a small square of non-stick or waxed paper is placed on top. The flower is then piped on to the paper, the nail being easily rotated as each petal is piped.

Specialist equipment

Cake Basics

Cake recipes vary greatly, not only by the methods used to make the cakes but also in the balance of the various ingredients. The basic aim of most cake making is to incorporate air into the ingredients so that during baking the mixture rises and a light texture is formed.

There are no secrets to making a cake worthy of being iced or decorated – just following a few simple golden rules will ensure successful results. Once made, these unassuming cakes may be turned into masterpieces simply by filling, icing and decorating.

Cake-making golden rules

- Always make sure you have the correct tin shape and size according to the recipe you are making. By substituting a different cake tin size or shape, you'll not only affect the final baking time but also the volume, texture and appearance of the cake.
- Ensure the tin is properly prepared and lined for baking the recipe you have chosen to make. Different cake mixtures require specific tin treatments to ensure even cooking and a regular shape.
- Check that you have all the necessary ingredients stated in the recipe and that they are at the right temperature.
- Measure all the ingredients accurately using scales, measuring spoons and a measuring jug. Always work in either metric or imperial, to prevent mistakes when weighing or measuring.
- Use the egg sizes stated in the recipe. Substituting different sizes can affect the balance of the cake mixture.
- Sifting dry ingredients together helps not only to aerate, but also to disperse lumps. Store flours and raising agents in well-sealed packets or airtight containers in a cool, dry place.
- When making cakes by hand, beat well with a wooden spoon until the mixture is light and fluffy (this will only be possible if your butter is at the correct temperature). If the cake is being made in a food processor, freestanding mixer or using a hand-held electric whisk, be careful not to over-process or over-beat the mixture. If over-beaten, the mixture can over-rise in the oven, then collapse and dip in the centre during baking.

- Always scrape down the mixture with a spatula during mixing (remember to turn off any electric mixers first).
- If ingredients have to be folded into a cake mixture, use a large metal spoon, which will cut cleanly through the mixture. Keep scooping down to the bottom of the bowl, then turning the mixture on top of itself, while at the same time giving the bowl a quarter twist. Continue folding in this fashion just until the ingredients are combined – do not be tempted to over-fold the cake mixture or it will lose air, resulting in a heavy cake.
- If making larger cakes, check first that your oven is big enough. There should be at least 5cm (2 inches) oven space all around the cake tin to ensure it cooks evenly.
- Before any baking, check the temperature of your oven is correct by investing in an oven thermometer. These are inexpensive and available at any cookware shop. Check your oven is preheated to the correct temperature stated in the recipe.
- Never be tempted to open the oven door before at least three-quarters of the specified baking time has passed. By opening the oven too soon, the heat will escape and the cake will sink.
- The temperature of your cake ingredients and kitchen can also cause the baking time to vary. If conditions are cold, the mixture will take longer to cook. Similarly, if it is a very hot day, then baking will be slightly quicker.
- Always check the cake is cooked 5–10 minutes before the given baking time, just in case the oven is a little fast.

Ingredients

There are limited ingredients in cake making, so it is important to use the highest quality you can, and ensure that they are at the right temperature.

Fat

Unsalted butter generally gives the best results in most cake recipes. Margarine can be substituted in many recipes, although it doesn't lend such a good flavour. Low-fat spreads, with their high water content, are not suitable. For most cake recipes, you need to use the fat at room temperature. If necessary, soften it (cautiously) in the microwave.

Eggs

Eggs should be stored in the fridge in their box, but used at room temperature; if taken straight from the fridge they are more likely to curdle a cake mixture. Make sure you use the correct size – unless otherwise stated, medium eggs should be used in all the recipes.

How to test whether your eggs are fresh

Eggs frequently outlast their stated best before date, so do this test to see if they are still usable. Fill a bowl with cold water. One by one put your eggs into the water. Fresh eggs will sink to the bottom and lie either on their side or on their tip. If the egg floats it has gone off, so discard it.

Sugar

Lots of sugars can be used in cake making. Caster sugar (either white or golden), icing sugar, light and dark soft brown sugars and light or dark brown muscovado sugars are all common. Unrefined sugars give the best flavour.

Flour

Both plain and self-raising white flours are commonly used in cake making. Wholemeal flours give a denser texture and nuttier flavour. As white and wholemeal flours behave slightly differently when it comes to liquid absorption, never simply substitute wholemeal flour in a recipe stating plain flour.

How to turn plain flour into self-raising flour

Sift together 125g (4oz) plain flour and 1 tsp baking powder to make self-raising flour.

Baking powder

This is a raising agent consisting of an acid, usually cream of tartar, and an alkali, such as bicarbonate of soda. It is activated when it gets wet and produces carbon dioxide. This expands during baking and makes cakes and breads rise. Some baking powders are also heat activated.

Nuts

Some nuts can be bought ready prepared, others need preparation. After nuts have been shelled, they are still coated with a thin, papery skin, which although edible, tastes a little bitter. This is easier to remove if the nuts are blanched or toasted.

To blanch Put the shelled nuts into a bowl and cover with boiling water. Leave for 2 minutes, then drain. Remove the skins by rubbing the nuts in a teatowel or squeezing them between your thumb and index finger.

To toast Toasting nuts improves their flavour. Preheat the oven to 200°C (180°C fan oven) mark 6. Put the shelled nuts on a baking sheet in a single layer and toast for 8–15 minutes in the oven until the skins are beginning to toast. When cool enough to handle, remove the skins by rubbing the nuts in a teatowel or squeezing them between your thumb and index finger.

To chop Nuts are usually used chopped and the quickest way to achieve this is to pulse them in a food processor. Alternatively, chop them on a board with a cook's knife.

Dried fruit

Dried fruits are classified into vine fruits and tree fruits. Their moisture content is reduced by drying and the character of the fruits changes completely, becoming wrinkled, leathery and sweet. Always check on the packet whether the dried fruit needs any preparation or whether it is ready to eat.

Essences and extracts

Essences and extracts with flavours such as vanilla and almond make frequent appearances in cake making. Extracts are, in general, higher quality than essences and deliver a more natural flavour. If using essences, look for ones labelled 'natural', rather than 'flavouring'.

Techniques

A variety of methods of cake can be prepared using three basic techniques: creaming (see Victoria Sandwich, page 30), all-in-one (see Fairy Cakes, page 150), and whisking (see Whisked Sponge, page 31). These straightforward basic recipes can be adapted in several ways.

Lining tins

Unless otherwise stated, line your tins with greaseproof paper (use baking parchment for roulades or meringues). This will help stop the cake sticking to the sides of the tin or burning. Lightly grease the inside of the tin first to help keep the paper in place. Apply the butter or oil with kitchen paper – do not thickly grease the edges of the cake, you need just enough to hold the paper in place. Once the tin is lined, grease the paper lightly.

Lining a square tin

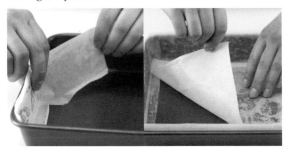

Lining a square tin

This method works well for larger square tins. For small tins, rather than cutting four side panels, use one long strip.

1 Put the tin base-down on greaseproof paper and draw around it. Cut out the square just inside the drawn line. Next, measure the length and depth of one of the sides of the tin. Cut four strips of greaseproof paper to this length, each about 2cm (¾ inch) wider than the depth of the tin. Fold up one of the long edges of each strip by 1cm (½ inch).

2 Lightly grease the inside of the tin with butter. Position the four strips in the tin, with the folded edge lying on the bottom. Next, lay the square on the bottom of the tin, then lightly grease the paper, taking care not to move the side strips.

Lining a round tin

Lining a round tin

1 Put the tin base-down on greaseproof paper and draw a circle around its circumference. Cut out the circle just inside the drawn line.

2 Cut a long strip about 2cm (¾ inch) wider than the depth of the tin, and long enough to wrap around the outside of the tin. Fold up one long edge of the strip by 1cm (½ inch). Make cuts, spacing them about 2.5cm (1 inch) apart, through the folded edge of the strip(s) up to the fold line.

3 Lightly grease the inside of the tin with butter. Press the strip to the inside of the tin, making sure the snipped edges sit on the bottom. Trim any overlap once inside the tin.

4 Lay the circle in the bottom of the tin, then lightly grease the paper.

Lining a Swiss roll tin

Use this method for a Swiss roll or any other shallow baking tin.

1 Put the tin base down in the centre of a large sheet of greaseproof paper or baking parchment and trim the paper so that it is 2.5cm (1 inch) wider than the tin on all sides. Still with the tin on the paper, cut from one corner of the paper to the closest corner of the tin. Repeat with the remaining corners.

2 Lightly grease the inside of the tin with butter. Fit the paper into the tin, neatly pressing into the corners. Lightly grease the paper.

Alternatively you can cut into the corners of the paper once it has been pressed into the tin.

Lining a Swiss roll tin

Lining a loaf tin

1 Cut out a sheet of greaseproof paper the same length as the base of the tin and wide enough to cover both the base and the long sides. Now cut another sheet to the same width as the base and long enough to cover both the base and the ends of the tin.

2 Lightly grease the inside of the tin with butter. Press the strips into position, making sure they fit snugly into the corners. Lightly grease with butter.

Lining shaped tins

1 Put the tin base down on greaseproof paper. Draw around the base following the tin shape and cut out.

2 Measure and cut a strip of greaseproof paper to fit around the outside of the tin. Lightly grease the inside of the tin with butter, then line the base and sides with the paper and grease again.

Lining a loaf tin

Lining shaped tins

Baking cakes

All recipes will give a guideline for the baking time, but oven temperatures can vary, depending on your oven, so make sure you use an oven thermometer for accurate baking and test the cake properly before taking it out of the oven.

- Always preheat your oven to the specified temperature, taking into account whether you will be using the conventional or fan temperature.
- It is important to bake the cake mixture as soon as you have put it into the tin or liners, as the raising agents will start to react straight away.
- Once the cake is in the oven (the middle shelf is usually best), resist the temptation to open the door for at least the first three-quarters of the stated time in the recipe, as a sudden gush of cold air will make a part-baked cake sink.
- If your cake appears to be browning too quickly, cover the top loosely with greaseproof or parchment paper.

Testing if cakes are cooked

Ovens vary and the time given in the recipe might be too short or too long to correctly cook what you are baking. So always test to ensure a successful result.

Testing sponges

Gently press the centre of the sponge. It should feel springy. If your fingers leave a depression, the cake needs to be returned to the oven. Retest every 5 minutes.

Alternatively, a skewer inserted into the centre of the cake should come out clean. If it is a whisked sponge (such as a Genoese), then simply do the finger test, as skewering the cake can cause it to sink. Another test for a whisked sponge is that the cake should be just shrinking away from the sides of the tin.

Testing fruit cakes

Insert a skewer into the centre of the cake, then pull it out. If it comes out clean, the cake is ready. If any mixture sticks to the skewer, the cake is not done yet. Put it back into the oven for 5–10 minutes more, then test again with a (wiped) clean skewer.

Cooling cakes

Always follow the cooling instructions stated in the recipe. If certain cakes are left for too long in the tin, they will sweat. Most fruit cakes, on the other hand, should be left to cool completely in the tin to help them stabilise. Make sure all cakes are completely cool before icing or storing.

Testing sponges

Testing fruit cakes

Calculating servings from a cake

Before you bake any cake it is worth estimating how many it will feed. A smaller birthday or occasion cake can usually be cut into wedges. Servings of larger celebration or novelty cakes tend to be smaller – more like a finger of cake than a wedge, so estimating how many the cake will feed is crucial.

Estimating how many servings from a cake

Cakes are only cut into wedges when they are smaller, and it's quite easy to estimate without a guide. However, if cutting into small fingers of cake, rather than wedges, whether the cake tin is round, square, heart-shaped or hexagonal, by following this simple method you will be able to estimate how many the cake will feed prior to baking.

Draw around the cake tin on a piece of paper. Next, draw parallel lines inside the outline of the cake, spacing about 2.5cm (1 inch) apart (or thinner if you desire). Now divide each 'cake slice' into 4cm (1½ inch) pieces, or to the size you require. Count up the portions in your diagram and you have your estimate as to how many the finished cake will feed. But remember that if the cake is very deep it will feed more.

It's worth remembering that a square cake is larger than a round cake of the same size, and will yield more servings. Unusual-shaped cakes may vary in the quantities they yield, so use the same method to estimate portions before baking. The chart below shows rough portions as these will vary depending on how the cake is sliced and the depth of the cake.

note

Sometimes if time is short or the cake has to be produced on a small budget, it is quite acceptable to have just one beautifully iced and decorated cake for the centrepiece. The remaining cake required may be made as one large slab cake with simpler icing. This will not be seen by the guests but may be cut into servings as above.

Reception cake portion chart

This is based on cake pieces being about 2.5cm (1 inch) thick and 4cm (1½ inches) long

Cake sizes	Round cake portions	Square cake portions
12.5cm (5in)	16	20
15cm (6in)	25	30
18cm (7in)	36	42
20.5cm (8in)	45	56
23cm (9in)	64	72
25.5cm (10in)	81	90
28cm (11in)	100	120
30.5cm (12in)	120	140

Basic cake mixtures and techniques

Cake recipes vary greatly, not only by methods used to make the cakes but also by the balance of the various ingredients – so make sure you follow the recipes closely and you'll be guaranteed good results.

Rich fruit cakes freeze well, so if you want to make yours well in advance this is the best way to store it. Once completely cooled, leave the cake in its lining paper, then wrap in a double layer of greaseproof paper and overwrap in a double layer of foil. Freeze for up to six months. To thaw, leave the cake in its wrapping at room temperature until completely thawed.

As fruit cakes tend to be stored for extended periods of time, care must be taken to ensure that they are made in a spotlessly clean environment. All utensils must be clean and well cared for; ingredients must be freshly purchased; tins carefully lined and prepared.

Quick Mix Rich Fruit Cake

cuts into 16 larger slices

Preparation: 30 minutes
Cooking time: 2½ hours, plus cooling

175g (6oz) unsalted butter, cubed, plus extra to grease
1kg (2¼lb) mixed dried fruit
100g (3½oz) ready-to-eat prunes, roughly chopped
50g (2oz) ready-to-eat dried figs, roughly chopped
100g (3½oz) dried cranberries
2 balls preserved stem ginger in syrup, grated (1 tbsp syrup reserved)
grated zest and juice of 1 orange
175ml (6fl oz) brandy
2 splashes Angostura bitters
175g (6oz) dark muscovado sugar
200g (7oz) self-raising flour
½ tsp ground cinnamon
½ tsp freshly grated nutmeg
½ tsp ground cloves
4 medium eggs, beaten

Per slice
277 cals; 11g fat (of which 6g saturates);
38g carbohydrate; 0.2g salt

Rich fruit cake is suitable for any celebration cake since it can be made in advance and is substantial enough to be covered with almond paste and sugarpaste or royal icing. This rich fruit cake is a quick mix recipe.

1 Preheat the oven to 150°C (130°C fan oven) mark 2. Grease a 20.5cm (8 inch) round, deep cake tin and line the base and sides with a double thickness of greaseproof paper. Once the tin is lined, grease the paper lightly.

2 Put all the dried fruit into a large pan and add the ginger, reserved ginger syrup, the orange zest and juice, brandy and Angostura bitters. Bring to the boil, then simmer for 5 minutes. Add the butter and sugar and heat gently to melt. Stir occasionally until the sugar dissolves. Take the pan off the heat and leave to cool for a couple of minutes.

3 Add the flour, spices and beaten eggs and mix well. Pour the mixture into the prepared tin and level the surface. Now make a slight depression in the centre of the cake mix (to prevent it doming while baking). Wrap the outside of the tin in brown paper and secure with string to protect the cake during cooking. Put the tin on a baking sheet and bake for 2–2½ hours – cover the top with greaseproof paper after about 1½ hours – until the cake is firm to the touch and a skewer inserted into the centre comes out clean.

4 Cool completely in the tin. Once cool, take out of tin (leaving the lining paper around the cake). Wrap the cake in a double layer of greaseproof, then overwrap in a double layer of foil.

Traditional Rich Fruit Cake

cuts into 16 larger slices

Preparation: 30 minutes, plus overnight soaking

Cooking time: 3½ hours, plus cooling

450g (1lb) currants

200g (7oz) sultanas

200g (7oz) raisins

150g (5oz) glacé cherries

75g (3oz) chopped mixed peel

75g (3oz) flaked almonds

a little grated lemon zest

1 tbsp brandy

275g (10oz) unsalted butter

350g (12oz) plain flour

½ tsp mixed spice

½ tsp ground cinnamon

275g (10oz) soft brown sugar

5 medium eggs, beaten

Per slice

497 cals; 19g fat (of which 9.7g saturates); 80g carbohydrate; 0.4g salt

This second rich fruit cake recipe requires overnight soaking of the fruit. As mentioned before, rich fruit cakes can be made well in advance, and stored until needed. If you like, after the cake has matured for two weeks, you can prick the top all over with a metal skewer and sprinkle with 1–2 tbsp brandy. Leave this to soak in, then rewrap and store it as before. You can feed the cake like this every couple of weeks (there is no need to prick extra holes).

1 Put the currants, sultanas, raisins, glacé cherries, mixed peel, flaked almonds, lemon zest and brandy into a large non-aluminium bowl (glass or ceramic is best, as this won't react with the fruit). Mix well together, then cover with clingfilm and leave to soak overnight in a cool place.

2 When the fruit has soaked, grease a 20.5cm (8 inch) round, deep cake tin and line the base and sides with a double thickness of greaseproof paper. Grease the paper lightly. Tie a double band of brown paper around the outside of the tin (to protect the cake from burning while baking). Preheat the oven to 150°C (130°C fan oven) mark 2.

3 Sift the flour, mixed spice and cinnamon together into a separate large bowl. Add the butter, sugar and eggs. Mix together with a hand-held electric whisk until smooth and glossy – about 1 minute.

4 Using a large metal spoon or spatula, fold the soaked fruit into the flour mixture and continue folding until the fruit is evenly distributed. Spoon the mixture into the prepared tin and level the surface. Give the tin a few sharp bangs on a work surface to remove any air pockets. Now make a slight depression in the centre of the cake mix (to prevent it doming while baking).

5 Put the tin on a baking sheet and cook in the middle of the oven for 3–3½ hours – cover the top with greaseproof paper after about 1½ hours – until the cake is firm to the touch and a skewer inserted into the centre comes out clean.

6 Cool completely in the tin. Once cool, take out of the tin (leaving the lining paper around the cake). Wrap the cake in a double layer of greaseproof paper, then overwrap in a double layer of foil.

Quantities and sizes for Traditional Rich Fruit Cake

When baking large cakes, 25.5cm (10in) and upwards, it is advisable to reduce the oven heat to 130°C (110°C fan oven) mark 1 after two-thirds of the baking time.

CAKE TIN SIZE	12.5cm (5in) square 15cm (6in) round	15cm (6in) square 18cm (7in) round	18cm (7in) square 20.5cm (8in) round	20.5cm (8in) square 23cm (9in) round
Currants	225g (8oz)	350g (12oz)	450g (1lb)	625g (1lb 6oz)
Sultanas	100g (3½oz)	125g (4½ oz)	200g (7oz)	225g (8oz)
Raisins	100g (3½oz)	125g (4½ oz)	200g (7oz)	225g (8oz)
Glacé cherries	50g (2oz)	75g (3oz)	150g (5oz)	175g (6oz)
Mixed peel	25g (1oz)	50g (2oz)	75g (3oz)	100g (3½oz)
Flaked almonds	25g (1oz)	50g (2oz)	75g (3oz)	100g (3½oz)
Lemon zest, grated	a little	a little	a little	¼ lemon
Brandy	1 tbsp	1 tbsp	1–2 tbsp	2 tbsp
Softened unsalted butter	150g (5oz)	175g (6oz)	275g (10oz)	350g (12oz)
Plain flour	175g (6oz)	215g (7½oz)	350g (12oz)	400g (14oz)
Mixed spice	¼ tsp	½ tsp	½ tsp	1 tsp
Cinnamon	¼ tsp	½ tsp	½ tsp	1 tsp
Soft brown sugar	150g (5oz)	175g (6oz)	275g (10oz)	350g (12oz)
Medium eggs, beaten	2½	3	5	6
Baking time (approx.)	2½–3 hours	3–3½ hours	3½ hours	4 hours
Weight when cooked	1.1kg (2½lb)	1.5kg (3¼lb)	2.1kg (4¾lb)	2.7kg (6lb)

CAKE TIN SIZE (continued)	23cm (9in) square 25.5cm (10in) round	25.5cm (10in) square 28cm (11in) round	28cm (11in) square 30.5cm (12in) round	30.5cm (12in) square 33cm (13in) round
Currants	775g (1lb 12oz)	1.1kg (2½lb)	1.5kg (3¼lb)	1.7kg (3¾lb)
Sultanas	375g (13oz)	400g (14oz)	525g (1lb 3oz)	625g (1lb 6oz)
Raisins	375g (13oz)	400g (14oz)	525g (1lb 3oz)	625g (1lb 6oz)
Glacé cherries	250g (9oz)	275g (10oz)	350g (12oz)	425g (15oz)
Mixed peel	150g (5oz)	200g (7oz)	250g (9oz)	275g (10oz)
Flaked almonds	150g (5oz)	200g (7oz)	250g (9oz)	275g (10oz)
Lemon rind, grated	¼ lemon	½ lemon	½ lemon	1 lemon
Brandy	2–3 tbsp	3 tbsp	4 tbsp	6 tbsp
Softened unsalted butter	500g (1lb 2oz)	600g (1lb 5oz)	800g (1lb 12oz)	950g (2lb 2oz)
Plain flour	600g (1lb 5oz)	700g (1½lb)	825g (1lb 13oz)	1kg (2¼lb)
Mixed spice	1 tsp	2 tsp	2½ tsp	2½ tsp
Cinnamon	1 tsp	2 tsp	2½ tsp	2½ tsp
Soft brown sugar	500g (1lb 2oz)	600g (1lb 5oz)	800g (1lb 12oz)	950g (2lb 2oz)
Medium eggs, beaten	9	11	14	17
Baking time (approx.)	4½ hours	6 hours	6–6½ hours	6½ hours
Weight when cooked	3.8kg (8½lb)	4.8kg (10½lb)	6.1kg (13½lb)	7.4kg (16½lb)

Victoria Sandwich

Preparation: 20 minutes

Cooking time: about 25 minutes,
plus cooling

175g (6oz) unsalted butter, softened,
plus extra to grease

175g (6oz) caster sugar

3 medium eggs

175g (6oz) self-raising flour, sifted

3–4 tbsp jam (strawberry or raspberry is
most traditional)

icing or caster sugar

Per slice

445 cals; 21g fat (of which 11g saturates);
30g carbohydrate; 0.8g salt

variations

CHOCOLATE Replace 3 tbsp flour with
sifted cocoa powder. Sandwich the
cakes with vanilla or chocolate
buttercream (see page 48).

COFFEE Blend together 2 tsp instant coffee
granules with 1 tbsp boiling water.
Cool and add to the creamed mixture
with the eggs. Sandwich the cakes
together with vanilla or coffee
buttercream (see page 48).

CITRUS Add the finely grated zest of an
orange, lime or lemon to the raw cake
mixture. Sandwich the cakes together
with orange, lime or lemon
buttercream (see page 48).

A traditional English cake that can be made in different shapes and flavours to suit plain, fancy or novelty cakes. It is not structurally strong enough to support being baked into large or tiered cakes, but can be cut, layered and shaped well.

1 Preheat the oven to 190°C (170°C fan oven) mark 5. Grease two 18cm (7 inch) sandwich tins and base-line with greaseproof paper.
2 Put the butter and caster sugar into a large bowl and, using a hand-held electric whisk, beat together until pale and fluffy. Add the eggs one at a time, beating well after each addition – add a spoonful of the flour if the mixture looks like it is about to curdle.
3 Once the eggs are added, use a large metal spoon to fold in the remaining flour. Divide the mixture evenly between the tins and level the surface.
4 Bake in the centre of the oven for 20–25 minutes until the cakes are well risen and spring back when lightly pressed in the centre. Loosen the edges with a palette knife and leave in the tins for 10 minutes.
5 Turn out, remove the lining paper and leave to cool on a wire rack. Sandwich the two cakes together with jam and dust with icing sugar or sprinkle the top with caster sugar. Slice and serve.

Quantities and sizes for a Victoria Sponge

CAKE TIN SIZE	15cm (6in) round 12.5cm (5in) square	18cm (7in) round 15cm (6in) square	20.5cm (8in) round 18cm (7in) square
Butter, softened	125g (4oz)	175g (6oz)	225g (8oz)
Caster sugar	125g (4oz)	175g (6oz)	225g (8oz)
Medium eggs	2	3	4
Self-raising flour	125g (4oz)	175g (6oz)	225g (8oz)
Baking time	20 minutes	25 minutes	25–30 minutes

Whisked Sponge

cuts into 6–8 slices

Preparation: 25 minutes
Cooking time: about 25 minutes,
plus cooling

unsalted butter to grease
90g (3¼oz) plain flour, plus extra to dust
3 large eggs
125g (4oz) caster sugar

To assemble
3–4 tbsp strawberry, raspberry or apricot jam
125ml (4fl oz) whipping or double cream,
whipped (optional)
icing or caster sugar

Per slice
215–160 cals; 4–3g fat (of which 0.9–0.7g
saturates); 30–24g carbohydrate; 0.1g salt

A quick, easy and light sponge mixture suitable for gâteaux, Swiss rolls or birthday cakes. Low in fat (before filling!) and very fluffy. The mixture is whisked over hot water to help the eggs and sugar whisk to full volume. Note, though, that this classic almost fat-less sponge does not keep well and is best eaten on the day it is made.

1   Preheat the oven to 190°C (170°C fan oven) mark 5. Grease and base-line two 18cm (7 inch) sandwich tins, grease the paper lightly and dust the sides with a little flour.
2   Put the eggs and caster sugar into a large heatproof bowl and, using a hand-held electric whisk, beat until well blended. Put the bowl over a pan of hot water (making sure the base of the bowl doesn't touch the water) and whisk until the mixture is pale and creamy and thick enough to leave a trail on the surface when the whisk is lifted – about 5 minutes. Remove the bowl from the pan and carry on whisking until cool.
3   Sift half the flour over the mixture and, using a large metal spoon or spatula, fold it in very lightly (trying to knock out as little air as possible). Sift in the remaining flour and repeat the folding process until combined.
4   Pour the mixture into the prepared tins, tilting the tins to spread the mixture evenly (do not bang on the surface as this will knock out valuable air). Bake in the middle of the oven for 20–25 minutes until well risen and springy to the touch when lightly pressed in the centre (do not test with a skewer, as this can cause the cake to sink).
5   Turn the cakes out on to a wire rack to cool. When completely cool, peel off the lining paper and sandwich the cakes together with jam and whipped cream, if using. Dust with icing sugar or sprinkle the top with caster sugar. Serve in slices.

Genoese Sponge

cuts into 6 large slices

Preparation: 25 minutes
Cooking time: 25–30 minutes or 30–40 minutes, plus cooling

40g (1½oz) unsalted butter, plus extra to grease
65g (2½oz) plain flour, plus extra to dust
3 large eggs
75g (3oz) caster sugar
1 tbsp cornflour

To assemble
3–4 tbsp strawberry, raspberry or apricot jam
125ml (4fl oz) whipping cream, whipped (optional)
icing sugar or caster sugar

Per slice
302 cals; 17g fat (of which 9.6g saturates); 34g carbohydrate; 0.2g salt

A whisked sponge with the addition of melted butter to give the cake a moist, firm texture. It is ideal for making into small fancy cakes or layering for gâteaux.

1 Grease two 18cm (7 inch) sandwich tins or one 18cm (7 inch) round, deep cake tin, base-line with greaseproof paper and dust the sides with a little flour.
2 Put the butter into a small pan and heat gently to melt, then take off the heat and leave to stand for a few minutes to cool slightly.
3 Put the eggs and sugar into a bowl and, using a hand-held electric whisk, whisk until well blended. Place the bowl over a pan of hot water (making sure the base of the bowl doesn't touch the water) and whisk until the mixture is pale and creamy and thick enough to leave a trail on the surface when the whisk is lifted – about 5 minutes. Remove the bowl from the pan and whisk until cool.
4 Preheat the oven to 180°C (160°C fan oven) mark 4. Sift the plain flour and cornflour into the egg bowl, then carefully fold in using a large metal spoon (trying to knock out as little air as possible).
5 Pour the melted and cooled butter around the edges of the mixture, leaving any butter sediment behind in the pan. Very lightly, fold in the butter until it has been incorporated into the mixture. Pour into the tin(s).
6 Bake in the oven for 25–30 minutes for the sandwich tins, or 35–40 minutes for the deep tin, until well risen and the cakes spring back when lightly pressed. Loosen the cake edge and leave to cool for 10 minutes. Turn out and leave to cool completely on a wire rack.
7 When completely cool, peel off the lining paper, (halve the single cake) and sandwich together with jam and whipped cream, if using. Dust with icing sugar or sprinkle the top with caster sugar. Serve in slices.

Swiss Roll

cuts into 8 slices

Preparation: 25 minutes
Cooking time: 10–12 minutes, plus cooling

unsalted butter to grease
125g (4oz) caster sugar, plus extra to dust
125g (4oz) plain flour, plus extra to dust
3 large eggs

To assemble
caster sugar to sprinkle
125g (4oz) jam, warmed

Per slice
200 cals; 3g fat (of which 0.7g saturates); 41g carbohydrate; 0.9g salt

This delightfully springy sponge roll makes a wonderful centrepiece that's easy to slice and portion. Fill with your favourite jam to add flavour and colour.

1 Grease and line a 33 × 23cm (13 × 9 inch) Swiss roll tin (see page 23), then grease the paper lightly. Dust the paper with caster sugar and flour. Preheat the oven to 200°C (180°C fan oven) mark 6.
2 Put the eggs and sugar into a large heatproof bowl and, using a hand-held electric whisk, beat until well combined. Put the bowl over a pan of hot water (making sure the base of the bowl does not touch the water) and whisk until the mixture is pale and creamy and thick enough to leave a trail on the surface when the whisk is lifted – about 5 minutes. Remove the bowl from the pan and whisk until cool.
3 Sift half the flour over the mixture and, using a large metal spoon or spatula, fold it in very lightly. Sift in the remaining flour and gently fold in as before until combined. Carefully fold in 1 tbsp hot water.
4 Pour the mixture into the tin and tilt the tin to spread the mixture evenly. Bake for 10–12 minutes until pale golden, risen and springy to the touch.
5 Meanwhile, put a sheet of greaseproof paper larger than the Swiss roll tin on a damp teatowel. Dredge the paper with caster sugar. Quickly invert the cake on to the paper, then remove the tin and peel off the lining. If needed, trim off the crusty edges of the cake to neaten. Spread the jam over the top of the cake.
6 Using the greaseproof paper to help, roll up the cake from one of the short ends. Make the first turn as tight as possible so that the cake will roll evenly and have a good shape when finished. Once rolled, put seam-side down on a serving plate and sprinkle with caster sugar. Serve in slices.

Madeira Cake

cuts into 12 large slices

Preparation: 20 minutes
Cooking time: about 50 minutes,
plus cooling

275g (10oz) unsalted butter, softened,
plus extra to grease
175g (6oz) plain flour
175g (6oz) self-raising flour
275g (10oz) caster sugar
5 medium eggs, lightly beaten
lemon juice or milk

Per slice
260 cals; 14g fat (of which 8g saturates);
31g carbohydrate; 0.4g salt

This is a good moist plain cake that may be made as an alternative to rich or light fruit cake. It has a firm texture, therefore making it a good base for a celebration cake. There are many variations for flavouring this cake and, once covered with marzipan, royal icing or sugarpaste, it may be decorated for occasions.

1 Preheat the oven to 170°C (150°C fan oven) mark 3. Grease and line a 20.5cm (8 inch) round, deep cake tin, then grease the paper lightly.
2 Sift the flours together. Cream the butter and sugar together in a separate bowl until pale and fluffy. Gradually add the eggs, beating well after each addition.
3 Using a large metal spoon, fold the flours into the butter mixture, adding a little lemon juice or milk if necessary to give a dropping consistency.
4 Turn the mixture into the prepared tin and level the surface. Make a slight depression in the middle of the surface of the cake to ensure it doesn't mound/dome too much while baking.
5 Bake in the centre of the oven for about 1½–1¾ hours until the cake springs back lightly when pressed in the centre with a finger.
6 Leave the cake to cool in the tin for 15 minutes, then remove and cool completely on a wire rack. Wrap in clingfilm or foil and store in a cool place until required.

Quantities and sizes for Madeira cakes

To make a Madeira sponge cake follow the method above, choosing your tin size and corresponding ingredient amounts from the chart below:

CAKE TIN SIZE	15cm (6in) square 18cm (7in) round	18cm (7in) square 20.5cm (8in) round	20.5cm (8in) square 23cm (9in) round	23cm (9in) square 25.5cm (10in) round	25.5cm (10in) square 28cm (11in) round	28cm (11in) square 30.5cm (12in) round	30.5cm (12in) square 33cm (13in) round
Plain flour	125g (4oz)	175g (6oz)	225g (8oz)	250g (9oz)	275g (10oz)	350g (12oz)	450g (1lb)
Self-raising flour	125g (4oz)	175g (6oz)	225g (8oz)	250g (9oz)	275g (10oz)	350g (12oz)	450g (1lb)
Softened unsalted butter, or soft margarine	175g (6oz)	275g (10oz)	400g (14oz)	450g (1lb)	500g (1lb 2oz)	625g (1lb 6oz)	725g (1lb 10oz)
Caster sugar	175g (6oz)	275g (10oz)	400g (14oz)	450g (1lb)	500g (1lb 2oz)	625g (1lb 6oz)	725g (1lb 10oz)
Medium eggs	3	5	7	8	10	12	13
Lemon juice or milk	2 tbsp	3 tbsp	3½ tbsp	4 tbsp	4½ tbsp	5 tbsp	5½ tbsp
Baking time (approx.)	1¼–1½ hours	1½– 1¾ hours	1¾–2 hours	1¾–2 hours	2–2¼ hours	2¼–2½ hours	2½–2¾ hours

Marble Cake

cuts into 8 slices

Preparation: 25 minutes
Cooking time: about 45 minutes,
plus cooling and setting

175g (6oz) unsalted butter, softened,
plus extra to grease
175g (6oz) caster sugar
3 medium eggs, lightly beaten
125g (4oz) self-raising flour
1 tsp baking powder
50g (2oz) ground almonds
1 tbsp milk
2 tbsp cocoa powder, sifted

To ice
200g (7oz) plain dark chocolate
75g (3oz) butter

Per serving
579 cals; 40g fat (of which 22g saturates);
52g carbohydrate; 1g salt

Dragging a skewer through two contrasting-coloured cake mixes is the secret to making a professional-looking marble cake.

1 Preheat the oven to 190°C (170°C fan oven) mark 5. Grease a 900g (2lb) loaf tin and line with greaseproof paper (see page 23), then grease the paper lightly.

2 Using a hand-held electric whisk, cream the butter and sugar together until pale and fluffy. Gradually add the eggs, beating well after each addition.

3 Sift the flower and baking powder into the bowl, then add the ground almonds and milk. Using a large metal spoon, fold everything together. Spoon half the mixture into a clean bowl and fold through the sifted cocoa powder.

4 Spoon a dollop of each mixture alternately into the prepared tin until you have used up both mixtures. Bang the base of the tin once on a surface to level and remove any air bubbles. Draw a skewer backwards and forwards through the mixture a few times to create a marbled effect. Bake for 45 minutes–1 hour until a skewer inserted into the centre comes out clean.

5 Leave the cake to cool for 15 minutes in the tin, then lift out and cool completely on a wire rack.

6 To ice, melt the chocolate and butter together gently in a pan. Put the cake (without greaseproof paper) on a wire rack. Pour the chocolate over and leave to set before serving.

Cupcakes

makes 12 cupcakes
this recipe can also be used
to make 18 fairy cakes

Preparation: 20 minutes
Cooking time: 15 minutes, plus cooling

125g (4oz) self-raising flour, sifted

1 tsp baking powder

125g (4oz) caster sugar

125g (4oz) unsalted butter, softened

2 medium eggs

1 tbsp milk

For the icing and decoration

225g (8oz) icing sugar, sifted

assorted food colourings (optional)

sweets, sprinkles or coloured sugar
(optional)

Per cake

241 cals; 9.7 g fat (of which 5.7g saturates);
39g carbohydrate; 0.4g salt

variation

CHOCOLATE CUPCAKES Replace 2 tbsp of the
flour with the same amount of cocoa
powder. Stir 50g (2oz) chocolate chips,
sultanas or chopped dried apricots into
the raw cake mixture. Complete the
recipe.

A selection of decorated small or individual cakes always looks
pretty at teatime, whether a simple afternoon tea or as part of a
birthday or wedding spread. Many small cakes can be made from
a basic fairy cake mixture.

1 Preheat the oven to 180°C (160°C fan oven) mark 4. Put paper cupcake cases
   into 12 of the holes of a bun tin.
2 Put the flour, baking powder, caster sugar, butter, eggs and milk into a mixing
   bowl and beat with a hand-held electric whisk for 2 minutes or until the
   mixture is pale and very soft. Two-thirds fill each paper case with the mixture.
3 Bake for about 15 minutes or until golden brown and a skewer inserted into
   the centre comes out clean. Transfer to a wire rack (in their cases) and leave
   to cool completely.
4 Put the icing sugar into a bowl and gradually blend in 2–3 tbsp warm water
   until the icing is fairly stiff, but spreadable. Add a couple of drops of food
   colouring, if you like. Spread or pipe the icing over the cooled cakes and
   decorate with sweets, sprinkles or coloured sugar, if you like. Leave to set
   before serving.

to create a flat top on cupcakes and fairy cakes

For good results when icing cupcakes or fairy cakes they need to have a reasonably flat top.
Never over-fill the cases with cake mixture, they should be two-thirds full for cupcakes
and three-quarters full for fairy cakes. If they rise to a peak during baking, allow to cool
completely, then trim away the top with a sharp knife. Brush away any surplus crumbs
from the top of the cakes – otherwise the crumbs may mix in with the icing and spoil the
finished results. Never waste the trimmings – they can be frozen and used for trifles.

Cakes – what went wrong?

The cake has sunk in the middle
- The oven door was opened too soon
- The cake was under-baked
- The ingredients haven't been measured accurately
- The wrong cake tin may have been used

The cake is covered with little holes
- The cake was not put in the oven quickly enough
- The oven temperature was too low
- The raising agent was not mixed into the flour well enough

The cake has a cracked, domed top
- The oven temperature was too hot
- The cake was too near the top of the oven
- Insufficient liquid was used
- The baking tin was too small
- Too much raising agent was used

The cake has a dense texture
- The mixture curdled when the eggs were added
- Too much liquid was added
- The mixture was over-folded
- Too little raising agent was used or an ineffective raising agent that is past its 'use-by' date was used

The fruit has sunk to the bottom
- The mixture was too soft to support the weight of the fruit. This is liable to happen if the fruit was too sticky or wet

The cake edges are crunchy
- The baking tin was over-greased

The base and sides of the cake are damp and soggy
- The cake was left in the tin to cool

The cake has a sour flavour and/or a greenish tinge
- Too much bicarbonate of soda was used

Storing un-iced cakes

The storage time will vary depending on the cake, so always check the recipe.

- Everyday cakes such as sponge mixtures may be kept in an airtight container or simply wrapped in greaseproof paper and foil. This will ensure they keep moist and fresh with the exclusion of air. Make sure the cake is completely cold before you put it into the container. If you haven't a large enough container, then wrap the cake in a double layer of greaseproof paper and overwrap with foil.
- To store fruit cakes, leave the lining paper on the cakes, as this is sealed on to the surface during baking and keeps the cakes moist and fresh. Wrap the cake in a double layer of greaseproof or waxed paper and then a double layer of foil. Avoid putting rich fruit cakes in direct contact with foil – the fruit may react with it.

Store in a cool, dry place. Never seal a fruit cake in an airtight plastic container for long periods of time, as this may encourage mould growth.
- Light fruit cakes and Madeira cakes can be stored in the same way as rich fruit cakes but their keeping qualities are not as good.
- For long term storage, most cakes are better kept in the freezer in their wrappings, maintaining their flavour at peak condition until they are required. Thaw the cakes slowly in a cool dry place.
- It is unadvisable to freeze fully iced cakes (that have not yet been served), as the icing tends to weep on thawing, ruining its appearance.

Splitting cakes

Some recipes require cakes to be split into two or three layers before being sandwiched back together with a filling.

Splitting cakes with a knife

If you want a level top to your cake, then it is worth turning the cake upside down before splitting. Alternatively, if the cake has risen at the top, you can trim it level with a knife.

1 Leave the cake to cool completely before splitting, then place on a board or a turntable.

2 Using a large knife or large serrated knife with a shallow thin blade (such as a bread knife), mark the number of layers required on the side of the cake. Next, cut a small notch from the top to bottom on one side of the cake so you will know where to line the layers up. Alternatively, put two cocktail sticks above each other, one in the top half, one in the lower half

3 Using a sawing motion, cut midway between the top and bottom of the cake – or where needed to make your first layer. Turn the cake slowly while cutting, taking care to keep the blade parallel with the base, until you have cut all the way around the sides.

4 Cut through the central core and lift off the top of the cake. If your cake is delicate, you might want to slide a non-lipped cake base between the layers to support the top of the cake as you lift it off. Cut more layers as needed.

Splitting cakes with a knife

Supporting the cake layer with a non-lipped cake base

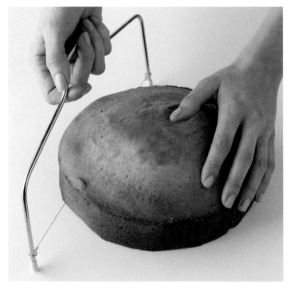

Splitting cakes with a cake cutting wire

Splitting cakes with a cake cutting wire

These easy-to-use cake wires are available from most specialist cake shops or via websites. They have a height-adjustable fine serrated blade, supported by a handle and stabilising feet to ensure regular cutting. Using gentle sawing motions you can cleanly and neatly cut a cake into multiple layers. The only constriction is the width of the tool, so make sure you buy one wider than your cake.

Filling cakes with icing or frosting

Fillings come in different textures, consistencies, flavours and colours. A filling is the essential part of assembling a layered cake or gâteaux, as it offers moisture, flavour and a way of sandwiching the layers back together to give the cake a good shape. Some fillings team better with some cakes than others – if a cake is light and delicate in texture, it needs to be filled with a light cream filling or frosting, while a more substantial cake will tolerate a richer type of filling. A light cake will not support a heavy filling, which can cause the cake to collapse and fall apart on slicing.

To fill a cake

Put the cake on a board and decide on the filling. Once decided, you need to get the consistency right. If the filling is too firm, it will pull the crumbs off the cake as you spread it or even rip it. If too soft, it will ooze out of the cake once it is sandwiched back together.

First dollop some of the filling in the middle of the cake, then spread with a metal knife (a palette knife is good, if you have one) that has briefly been dipped into a jug of hot water. Re-dip the knife as needed to obtain a smooth, level finish. Alternatively, pipe fillings such as buttercream or whipped cream to create an even finish.

Filling options include whipped (flavoured) cream, flavoured frostings, buttercreams, fudge icings and jams, which team well with cream, frosting and icings.

To fill a cake

To rebuild a cake

Once you have covered the base layer of your cake with filling, carefully position on the next layer of cake, using your cut notch or cocktail sticks to guide you. Repeat the filling and layering process as needed.

To rebuild a cake

Icing, Frosting & Covering Cakes

There are lots of options for covering cakes, depending on the finish you require. Each icing or frosting has its own characteristic texture, flavour, colour and consistency, and may be used to fill, cover and decorate cakes. Some icings are satin smooth and can be poured over the cake to give a smooth glossy finish, whereas other coverings may need spreading or swirling to give a textured appearance.

Covering a cake using basic icings

To cover a cake with a basic icing such as buttercream or glacé, first make sure your icing is well beaten, smooth and soft in texture, so that it does not pull up the surface crumbs of the cake as you spread it. Practise by spreading some on a board first.

Put the cake on a cake board and place it on the turntable, if using. Place a large spoonful of icing on top of the cake and use a palette knife to spread the icing smoothly over the top. Have a jug of hot water near you to quickly dip the knife into as the icing is spread, so that the icing does not stick to the palette knife (this works best if you clean the knife before dipping). Then add more icing to the sides and spread to obtain a good even surface. Either leave the surface smooth, or paddle the palette knife backwards and forwards to give a rippled effect.

Covering a cake

Glacé Icing

Makes 225g (8oz), enough to cover 12 cupcakes or 18 fairy cakes

225g (8oz) icing sugar
a few drops of vanilla or almond flavouring (optional)
2–3 tbsp boiling water
food colouring (optional)

note

Food colourings are available in liquid, paste or powder form (see page 57). Add gradually (using the tip of a cocktail stick if using food colouring pastes or powders) until the desired colour is achieved.

1 Sift the icing sugar into a bowl. Add a few drops of flavouring, if you like.
2 Using a wooden spoon, gradually stir in enough water until the mixture is the consistency of thick cream. Beat until white and smooth, and the icing is thick enough to coat the back of the spoon. Add colouring (a little at a time), if you like, and use immediately – or if you can't use immediately, cover the surface of the icing with clingfilm for up to 1 hour to prevent the icing from setting.

variations

ORANGE OR LEMON Replace the water with strained orange or lemon juice.
CHOCOLATE Sift 2 tsp cocoa powder in with the icing sugar.
COFFEE Flavour with 1 tsp coffee essence or dissolve 2 tsp instant coffee granules in 1 tbsp of the hot water.
MOCHA Dissolve 1 tsp cocoa powder and 2 tsp instant coffee granules in 1 tbsp of the boiling water.
ROSE WATER Use 2 tsp rose water instead of water.
LIQUEUR Replace 2–3 tsp of the water with the same amount of any liqueur.
COLOUR Add a few drops of liquid food colour, or for a stronger colour use a food colouring paste.

Royal Icing

Royal icing can be made to different consistencies depending on whether you are using it to ice your marzipan-covered cake (see page 52-3), do piping work (see page 60), or make run-out decorations (see page 64). It is a little time-consuming to make, but gives a sparkling, classical finish to your cake.

Makes 450g (1lb), enough to cover top and sides (one layer) of a 20.5cm (8 inch) round cake

2 medium egg whites
¼ tsp lemon juice
450g (1lb) icing sugar, sifted
1 tsp glycerine

Before you attempt to royal ice a celebration cake, it is worth investing in a turntable, a straight edge and side scraper (see page 17) to obtain a smooth, flat surface.

1 Put the egg whites and lemon juice into a large clean bowl. Stir to break up the egg whites.
2 Add sufficient icing sugar, mixing constantly, to form the consistency of un-whipped cream. Continue mixing and adding small quantities of icing sugar every few minutes until the desired consistency has been reached (see Consistencies, overleaf), mixing well and gently beating after each addition of icing sugar. The icing should be smooth, glossy and light. Do not add the sugar too quickly or it will produce a dull heavy icing. If making large quantities of icing, this stage is best completed in a freestanding mixer on low speed. Stir in the glycerine until well blended.
3 Allow the icing to settle before using it; cover the surface with a piece of damp clingfilm and seal well, excluding all the air.
4 Stir the icing thoroughly before use, as this will disperse the air bubbles, then adjust the consistency if necessary by adding more sifted icing sugar or egg white (see overleaf).

Royal icing consistencies

The skill of using royal icing and the results obtained are always determined by the consistency of the icing made.

Cake-covering (icing) consistency

Stir the icing well with a wooden spoon, then lift the spoon out of the icing. The icing on the spoon should form a fine point that just curves over at the end – this stage is known as 'soft peak'. This consistency spreads smoothly and evenly and creates a flat finish when a straight edge is pulled across the surface. It also pulls up into sharp or soft peaks when lifted with a palette knife, producing peaked icing.

Piping consistency

Stir the icing well with a wooden spoon, then lift the spoon out of the icing. The icing on the spoon should form a fine, sharp point – this stage is known as 'sharp peak'. This consistency will flow easily for piping and will retain the definite shape of the piping nozzle used. When piping from a very fine writing nozzle, the icing will need to be made slightly softer, to prevent aching wrists.

Run-out decoration consistency

Omit the glycerine when making royal icing for run-outs so that they dry hard and are easy to handle without breakages. A 'medium peak' icing consistency is used to pipe the outlines that retain the shape of the run-out. Icing the consistency of thick cream is used to fill in the shapes. This icing consistency flows with the help of a fine brush to fill in the run-outs, but holds a rounded shape within the piped lines.

How much royal icing to make

The quantity of royal icing needed to ice a cake varies according to how the icing is applied, the thickness and the number of layers needed. The chart below is just a guide for covering each cake with two or three thin layers of flat royal icing:

Caring for your royal icing

Make sure your bowl of royal icing is covered at all times to prevent the surface from drying into lumps. Using damp clingfilm to seal the surface is fine, or store an airtight container, as long as it is filled to the top with icing to exclude any air. Try to work with small quantities of icing in a separate bowl taken from the main batch of royal icing (making sure the main bowl is kept covered). This will prevent any crumbs or hard bits of icing creeping into the main batch.

Quantity of royal icing needed

Weight	Square cake	Round cake
450g (1lb)	12.5cm (5in) square	15cm (6in) round
700g (1½lb)	15cm (6in) square	18cm (7in) round
900g (2lb)	18cm (7in) square	20.5cm (8in) round
1.1kg (2½lb)	20.5cm (8in) square	23cm (9in) round
1.4kg (3lb)	23cm (9in) square	25.5cm (10in) round
1.6kg (3½lb)	25.5cm (10in) square	28cm (11in) round
1.8kg (4lb)	28cm (11in) square	30.5cm (12in) round
2kg (4½lb)	30.5cm (12in) square	33cm (13in) round

Sugarpaste

Sugarpaste (also known as 'fondant' icing) requires a completely different approach from that for royal icing. Sugarpaste gives cakes a softly rounded, smooth shape, rather than the sharp, crisp, classical lines of the traditionally royal iced cake. Being smooth, pliable and easy to use, high standards are achieved quickly with the help of specialist equipment. Sugarpaste can be bought ready to use in a variety of colours, or can easily be coloured at home with food colouring pastes – but it's worth bearing in mind that colouring large quantities of sugarpaste can be time-consuming.

Sugarpaste can be used to cover the most unusual-shaped cake, and even the least experienced cake decorator can achieve a smooth, well-covered cake with a professional finish. Sets of tools, cutters, crimpers and embossers are all available to produce different designs, patterns, flowers and finishes to cakes covered with sugarpaste.

If using shop-bought sugarpaste, which will keep for several months in its original packaging, it is a good idea to buy a small quantity first to see if you are happy with the texture and its handling qualities. Sugarpaste is also indispensable for making decorations such as sugar flowers, leaves and cut-out sugar pieces, and for modelling animals and figures (see pages 77–78).

To colour sugarpaste

When tinting sugarpaste at home, the more concentrated and less liquid food colouring pastes are best (see page 57). Knead food colouring into a small piece of the sugarpaste until you achieve a darker colour than required. Then knead the coloured piece into the remaining sugarpaste until the colour is even throughout. It is worth wearing gloves when tinting, as food colouring can stain your hands. If the sugarpaste becomes too sticky, then knead in a little sifted icing sugar.

Sugarpaste (fondant) Icing

Makes 550g (1¼lb), enough to cover an 18cm (7 inch) cake

1 medium egg white

2 tbsp liquid glucose

1 tsp vanilla extract or rose water

450g (1lb) icing sugar, sifted, plus extra to dust

1 Put the egg white, liquid glucose and flavouring into a clean bowl, blending with a wooden spoon to break up the egg white. Add the icing sugar and mix together until the icing begins to bind together. Knead with your fingers until the mixture forms into a rough ball.

2 Put the sugarpaste on a surface lightly dusted with sifted icing sugar and knead thoroughly until smooth, pliable and free from cracks.

3 If the sugarpaste is too soft to handle and is sticky, knead in some more sifted icing sugar until firm and pliable. Likewise, if the sugarpaste is dry and firm, knead in a little boiled water until the sugarpaste reaches the desired consistency.

4 Wrap the sugarpaste completely in clingfilm or store in a polythene bag with all the air excluded for 1 hour before using.

To make sugarpaste in a food processor

Whiz the icing sugar in a food processor for 30 seconds, then add the egg white, glucose and flavouring and whiz for 1–2 minutes until the mixture forms a ball. Wrap completely in clingfilm and store in a polythene bag with all the air excluded.

Covering a cake with frosting

Using frostings you can achieve both satin-smooth and textured finishes.
If you want a smooth finish, then the cake board underneath the cake needs
to be the same size, or slightly smaller, than the cake.

Frostings are often used while warm, so make sure they are at the right consistency – thick enough to coat the back of your spoon evenly. If too thick, the bowl will need to be placed over hot water to melt the frosting (alternatively, beat in a little water). If too slack, allow the frosting to cool and, as it does, the frosting will thicken. Pour the frosting all at once over the top of the cake and allow the frosting to fall over the sides – spread quickly with a wet palette knife to achieve good results. Now run the palette knife around the base of the cake board to neaten the edge and allow the covering to dry. At this stage, you can add flavour and texture to your frosted cake by coating the sides with toasted nuts, crushed amaretti biscuits or meringues, praline or grated chocolate.

Vanilla Frosting

Makes 175g (6oz), enough to cover the top and sides of an 18cm (7 inch) round cake

150g (5oz) icing sugar

5 tsp vegetable oil

1 tbsp milk

a few drops of vanilla extract

An all-in-one icing that's as easy to make as it is to use. Slightly softer than buttercream.

1 Sift the icing sugar into a bowl and, using a wooden spoon, beat in the oil, milk and vanilla extract until smooth. Use immediately.

Coffee Fudge Frosting

Makes 400g (14oz), enough to cover a 20.5cm (8 inch) cake

50g (2oz) unsalted butter

125g (4oz) soft light brown sugar

2 tbsp single cream or milk

1 tbsp coffee granules

200g (7oz) icing sugar, sifted

A spreadable, easy frosting that kids and adults will love.

1 Put the butter, soft light brown sugar and cream or milk into a pan. Dissolve the coffee in 2 tbsp boiling water and add to the pan. Heat gently until the sugar dissolves, then bring up to the boil and bubble briskly for 3 minutes.
2 Take the pan off the heat and gradually stir in the icing sugar. Beat well with a wooden spoon for 1 minute or until smooth.
3 Use the frosting immediately, spreading it over the cake with a wet palette knife, or dilute with a little water to use as a smooth coating.

variation

CHOCOLATE FUDGE FROSTING Omit the coffee. Add 75g (3oz) plain chocolate, chopped, to the pan with the butter at the beginning of step 1. Complete the recipe.

Seven-minute Frosting

Makes 175g (6oz), enough to cover an 18cm (7 inch) cake

1 medium egg white

175g (6oz) caster sugar

2 tbsp water

pinch of salt

pinch of cream of tartar

A fluffy, white quick-mix frosting.

1 Put all the ingredients into a heat proof bowl and whisk lightly using a hand-held electric whisk.
2 Put the bowl over a pan of hot water (making sure the base of the bowl does not touch the water) and heat gently, whisking constantly, until the mixture thickens sufficiently to stand in peaks – about 7 minutes.
3 Pour the frosting over the top of the cake and spread with a palette knife.

American Frosting

Makes 225g (8oz), enough to cover a 20.5cm (8 inch) cake

1 large egg white

225g (8oz) caster or granulated sugar

4 tbsp water

pinch of cream of tartar

A little tricky to make, so follow the recipe closely and you'll be rewarded with an icing you'll turn to time and again to cover all sorts of cakes.

1 Put the egg white into a large bowl and whisk until stiff with a hand-held electric whisk.
2 Put the sugar, water and cream of tartar into a pan. Heat gently, stirring until the sugar dissolves. Bring to the boil, without stirring, and boil until the sugar reaches 115°C (240°F) on a sugar thermometer.
3 Remove the syrup from the heat and immediately, when the bubbles subside, pour the syrup on to the egg white in a thin stream, whisking the mixture constantly. Continue whisking until thick and white, then leave to cool slightly.
4 When the mixture starts to go dull around the edges and is almost cold, pour quickly over the cake and spread evenly with a palette knife, swirling to create a nice effect.

Easy Whisked Icing

Makes 675g (1lb), enough to cover a 20.5cm (8 inch) almond paste-covered cake

3 medium egg whites

2 tbsp lemon juice

2 tsp glycerine

675g (1lb 7oz) icing sugar, sifted

Made in a matter of minutes, this quick-mix icing is ideal to create snowy Christmas cakes or white-peaked novelty cakes. Remember to factor in the drying time.

1 Put the egg whites into a large bowl and whisk until frothy using a hand-held electric whisk – there should just be a layer of bubbles across the top. Add the lemon juice, glycerine and 2 tbsp icing sugar and whisk until smooth.
2 Whisk in the remaining icing sugar, a little at a time, until the mixture is smooth, thick and forming into soft peaks.
3 Using a palette knife, smooth half the icing over the top and sides of the cake, then repeat using the remaining icing to cover. Use the palette knife to smooth or form the icing into peaks. Leave to dry in a cool place for at least 48 hours.

Buttercream

Makes 250g (9oz), enough
to cover the top and sides of
a 20.5cm (8 inch) cake

75g (3oz) unsalted butter, softened

175g (6oz) icing sugar, sieved

a few drops of vanilla extract

1–2 tbsp milk or water

This easy and classic recipe can be used as a filling or an icing.
Perfect for spreading or piping on top of cupcakes, or for filling and
covering cakes.

1 Put the butter into a bowl and beat with a wooden spoon or hand-held
electric whisk until light and fluffy.
2 Gradually stir in the icing sugar, followed by the vanilla and milk or water.
Beat well until light and smooth. Either use immediately or cover well with
clingfilm to exclude air.

variations

ORANGE, LEMON OR LIME Replace the vanilla extract with a little finely grated orange, lemon or
lime zest. Add a little juice from the fruit instead of the milk, beating well to avoid
curdling the mixture.
COFFEE Replace the vanilla extract with 2 tsp instant coffee granules dissolved in 1 tbsp
boiling water; cool before adding to the mixture.
CHOCOLATE Blend 1 tbsp cocoa powder with 2 tbsp boiling water and cool before adding to
the mixture.

Chocolate Ganache

Makes 225g (8oz), enough to
cover an 18cm (7 inch) round
cake

225g (8oz) good-quality plain dark chocolate
(with 60–70% cocoa solids)

250ml (9fl oz) double cream

Ever-popular, this ganache icing is ideal for covering cakes
for an elegant finish. Use ganache at room temperature as a
smooth coating for cakes, or chill it lightly until thickened
and use to fill meringues, choux buns or sandwich cakes.
This ganache is not hugely sweet, so if you are making for
children add 1 tbsp golden syrup to the chocolate bowl in step 1.

1 Roughly chop the chocolate and put into a medium heatproof bowl. Pour
the cream into a pan and bring to the boil.
2 As soon as the cream comes to the boil, pour it into the chocolate bowl
and stir gently until the chocolate has melted and the mixture is smooth.
Set aside for 5 minutes.
3 Whisk the ganache until it begins to hold its shape. Used at room
temperature, the mixture should be the consistency of softened butter.

variations

COFFEE Stir in 1 tsp instant coffee (liquid or granules) or a shot of espresso when melting
the chocolate.
SPICES Add a pinch of ground cinnamon, crushed cardamom seeds, a pinch of cayenne
pepper or freshly grated nutmeg to the melting chocolate.
VANILLA Stir in tsp vanilla extract when melting the chocolate.
RUM, WHISKY OR COGNAC Stir in about 1 tsp alcohol when melting the chocolate.
BUTTER Stir in 25g (1oz) butter towards the end of heating the milk.

Apricot Glaze

Used to brush over cakes before applying marzipan or to give fruit finishes on gâteaux and cakes a lustrous shine. It is always a good idea to make a large quantity of apricot glaze, especially when making a celebration cake. Never try to cheat by simply painting the cake with apricot jam, as this might cause fermentation between the cake and the almond paste.

Makes 450g (1lb) apricot glaze

450g (1lb) apricot jam
2 tbsp water

1 Put the jam and water into a pan, heat gently, stirring occasionally until melted.
2 Boil the jam rapidly for 1 minute, then strain through a fine sieve – pushing as much mixture through as possible.
3 Pour the glaze into a clean, sterilised jar. Seal with a clean lid and cool. It can be chilled for up to two months.
4 To use, brush over cakes before applying almond paste, or use to glaze fruit finishes. If the consistency is a little stiff, then stir in a few drops of boiled water.

Almond paste and marzipan

There is confusion as to the difference between almond paste and marzipan. Both are an amalgamation of ground almonds, caster or icing sugar, eggs and flavourings. The difference is in the varying proportion of ground almonds used in relation to the other ingredients. Usually, almond paste consists of a minimum of 50% almonds, whereas marzipan consists of about 30% ground almonds and has a higher proportion of sugar.

The consistency, texture and colour varies depending on how they are both made, but the end result is used for covering cakes to preserve them, to keep in the moisture and flavour, to prevent the cake leaking into the icing, and to give a flat surface for royal icing or sugarpaste. Marzipan is the one you should use for modelling since it gives a smooth finish (almond paste would just crack or become greasy).

Home-made almond paste has a wonderful taste and texture of its own. Care must be taken not to over-knead or over-handle the mixture, as this encourages the oil to flow from the ground almonds, making the paste greasy (and the oils will eventually seep through the final layer of icing).

Ready-made almond paste is available, but slightly harder to find.

Ready-made marzipan has a slightly firmer texture and generally comes in white or yellow varieties. Both give the same finished result, so choose depending on your preference – but remember that the yellow may show through if you are planning on only giving your cakes a thin layer of icing. White marzipan is better for modelling, as it takes on colour better. Always wrap any spare marzipan in a polythene bag to prevent it from drying out.

Almond Paste

Makes 900g–1kg (2–2¼lb)

225g (8oz) icing sugar

225g (8oz) caster sugar

450g (1lb) ground almonds

1 tsp vanilla extract

2 medium egg whites, lightly beaten

2 tsp lemon juice

As home-made almond paste contains raw eggs, it is best not fed to the very young, the old, or to pregnant women. As an alternative to raw egg whites, use water mixed with a little sherry or brandy and the lemon juice to bind the mixture.

1 Sift the icing sugar into a bowl and mix in the caster sugar and ground almonds.
2 Add the vanilla extract, egg whites and lemon juice, and mix to a stiff dough. Knead lightly, then shape into a ball. Cover until ready to use.

To cover a cake with marzipan

To marzipan a cake ready for icing is a very exacting process, as the finished marzipanned shape of the cake determines the smoothness of the icing. When covering a cake for royal icing, the shape needs to be clean, sharp and smooth – hence the covering process is a little more involved. On the other hand, when covering a cake for sugarpaste, it is necessary to smooth the marzipan to the contours and shape of the cake to ensure a more rounded appearance.

Quantities for covering a cake with marzipan

You can generally use the same principle when covering a cake with almond paste, but this covering is more likely to tear, so don't panic if you have to do some fixing.

CAKE SIZES	12.5cm (5in) square 15cm (6in) round	15cm (6in) square 18cm (7in) round	18cm (7in) square 20.5cm (8in) round	20.5cm (8in) square 23cm (9in) round	23cm (9in) square 25.5cm (10in) round	25.5cm (10in) square 28cm (11in) round	28cm (11in) square 30.5cm (12in) round	30.5cm(12in) square 33cm (13in) round
Marzipan or almond paste	450g (1lb)	550g (1¼lb)	700g (1½lb)	800g (1¾lb)	1kg (2¼lb)	1.1kg (2½lb)	1.25kg (2¾lb)	1.6kg (3½lb)

To marzipan a cake for royal icing

1 Unwrap the cake. Remove the lining paper. Roll the cake top with a rolling pin to give a flat surface. Brush the top of the cake evenly with apricot glaze (see page 49). Dust a work surface lightly with sifted icing sugar.

2 Using two-thirds of the specified marzipan for your cake (see marzipan quantity chart opposite), knead it and roll out to a thickness of 5mm (¼ inch) to roughly match the shape of the top of the cake – make sure the marzipan is not sticking to the surface. Now invert the cake on to the centre of the marzipan.

3 Using a small knife, trim off excess marzipan around the cake to within 1cm (½ inch) of the cake. Using a palette knife, push the marzipan level with the sides of the cake until all the edges are neat.

4 Invert the cake (marzipan up) and put on to a cake board about 5cm (2 inches) larger than the cake. Brush the sides with apricot glaze. Knead the trimmings and remaining one-third of marzipan together, taking care not to include any cake crumbs.

5 Measure the width and length of the cake first. Roll out the marzipan to a thickness of 5mm (¼ inch) and cut out the side panel(s) to width and length. Reroll the trimmings as necessary.

6 Carefully stick the marzipan on to the side of the cake and, using your hands dusted in icing sugar or cornflour, or with the help of a cake smoother, smooth the joins. Leave the cake to harden for 24–48 hours in a cool, dry place before icing.

To marzipan a cake for sugarpaste

1 Unwrap the cake and remove the lining paper. Place the cake on a matching shaped cake board about 5cm (2 inches) larger than the cake. Roll the top with a rolling pin to give a flat surface. Brush the top and sides of the cake with apricot glaze (see page 49), then dust a work surface lightly with sifted icing sugar.

2 Knead the specified marzipan quantity for your cake until smooth, then roll out to 5mm (¼ inch) thickness until the marzipan is large enough to cover the top and sides of the cake, allowing about 5–7.5cm (2–3 inches) extra all the way round.

3 Make sure the marzipan is not sticking to the surface, then roll it loosely around the rolling pin. Starting from one side of the cake, carefully unroll the marzipan on to the cake.

4 Working from the centre of the cake, carefully smooth the marzipan over the top of the cake, ensuring there are no trapped air pockets, then smooth down the sides. Lift the edges slightly to allow the marzipan to be eased in to fit the base of the cake without stretching or tearing the top edge.

5 Using a small knife, trim off the excess marzipan from the base, cutting down on to the board. Using clean, dry hands or a cake smoother, gently rub the cake in circular movements to give the marzipan a smooth, glossy, rounded finish. Leave the cake to harden for 24–48 hours in a cool, dry place before icing.

To marzipan a cake for royal icing

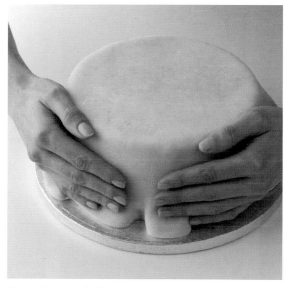

To marzipan a cake for sugarpaste

To cover a cake with marzipan   51

To royal ice a cake

Slightly different techniques need to be employed when icing a square or round cake, as detailed below.

To royal ice a square cake

By following this method your cake will have crisp, neat edges and a sparkling white finish. If you are less bothered about the finish, you can ice the entire cake in one go. Remember always to cover your royal icing with a damp piece of clingfilm when you are not using it to prevent it from drying out.

1 Make a quantity of royal icing to soft peak consistency (see page 44), then lay a damp piece of clingfilm in the bowl, touching the icing, to prevent it from drying out. Put the marzipanned (and dried) cake on a cake board, if it's not on one already. Have ready a large palette knife, a straight edge and a side scraper.

2 Using the palette knife, apply the royal icing to the top of the cake to cover the surface evenly. Paddle the icing back and forth in lines across the top to help eliminate air bubbles. Smooth as best as possible.

3 Holding each end of the straight edge, place it at the far side of the cake, just resting on the icing, then in one continuous movement pull across the top of the cake towards you. If the icing is not smooth enough, repeat the movement once again (using a clean straight edge). If the icing is getting a little thin, apply some more before using the straight edge. If you don't have a straight edge, then the edge of a large palette knife will work.

4 Use a clean palette knife to scrape any icing off the edges. Leave the top layer to dry for about 2 hours or overnight in a warm, dry place.

5 Put the cake on a turntable and, using a palette knife (a small one with a cranked handle is best), smoothly spread one side of the cake with royal icing to cover evenly. Paddle the icing back and forth to eliminate air bubbles. Remove excess icing from the dry icing edge on the top of the cake and from both corners, then pull a side scraper across the side to even the edge up. As before, if not neat enough repeat this process, adding more icing as necessary. Repeat the process on the opposite side and leave to dry for at least 2 hours.

6 Repeat the process to royal ice the remaining two opposite sides of the cake as before. Trim away excess icing from the top edge and corners of the cake. Leave to dry overnight.

7 Apply 1–3 further thin layers of royal icing, repeating the method as before, until the icing is smooth and flat. For the final coating, to obtain a really smooth finish, use icing with a slightly softer consistency.

8 Once you have finished icing the cake, ice the cake board, if needed, using a small palette knife and a side scraper.

To smooth royal icing using a straight edge

To cover the sides of the cake using a palette knife

To royal ice a round cake

To royal ice a round cake is similar to icing a square cake, but simpler and quicker.

1 Make a quantity of royal icing to soft peak consistency (see page 44), then lay a damp piece of clingfilm in the bowl, touching the icing, to prevent it from drying out. Put the marzipanned cake on a cake board if it's not on one already. Have ready a large palette knife, a straight edge and a side scraper.

2 Using a palette knife, spread some icing on top of the cake, enough to cover evenly. Paddle the icing back and forth to eliminate air bubbles. Remove any excess icing from the sides.

3 Holding each end of a straight edge, place it at the far side of the cake, just resting on the icing, then in one continuous movement pull across the top of the cake towards you. If the icing is not smooth enough, repeat the movement once again (using a clean straight edge). If the icing is getting a little thin, apply some more before using the straight edge. If you don't have a straight edge, the edge of a large palette knife will work. Remove any excess icing, then leave the top layer to dry for about 2 hours or overnight in a warm, dry place.

4 Put the cake on a turntable and use a palette knife to spread all around the side evenly with the royal icing, paddling it back and forward to eliminate air bubbles. When the side is covered, hold a cake scraper against the icing, resting the base of it on a cake board. With your other hand hold the edge of the cake board and turntable. Slowly turn the turntable while at the same time holding the side scraper against the icing, pulling it towards you in the opposite direction of the turning, to smooth the surface. Once you have gone round the cake, gradually pull off the side scraper (it will leave a 'pull off' mark). Neaten the top edge, then leave the cake to dry.

5 Repeat the process to cover the cake with 1–3 further thin layers of royal icing, using a slightly softer consistency for the final layer to give a smooth and sparkling finish.

6 Once you have finished icing the cake, ice the cake board, if needed, using a small palette knife and a side scraper.

> *tip*
>
> You can use fine sandpaper to buff down any imperfections (such as the 'pull off' mark) in the dry layers as you go along.

To smooth royal icing using a straight edge

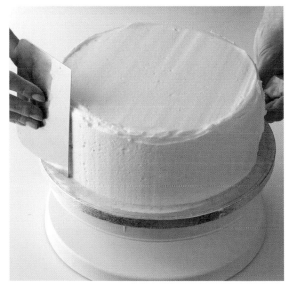

To smooth the sides of the cake using a cake scraper

To sugarpaste a cake

A smooth, rounded sugarpasted cake is a wonder to behold – and luckily not too difficult to achieve. There is a variety of techniques, some very easy indeed, which may be applied to cakes covered with sugarpaste to transform their appearance. Edges of cakes may be crimped or embossed, while the pliable paste may also be turned into frills and flounces to enhance the sides of a celebration cake.

To cover any shaped cake with sugarpaste

Always try to wear a white cotton apron over a white shirt or t-shirt when working with sugarpaste, so that coloured fabric particles don't fall into the icing.

1 Put the marzipanned cake on its matching cake board on a turntable. Brush the surface evenly with a little brandy or cooled boiled water. When covering a sponge cake with sugarpaste, spread with a thin layer of apricot jam or buttercream first instead of a layer of marzipan.
2 Dust the work surface and the rolling pin with a little sifted icing sugar. Roll out the sugarpaste to a 5mm (¼ inch) thickness to match the shape of the cake and large enough to cover the top and sides with a little extra all round.
3 Gently roll the sugarpaste on to the rolling pin, then lift over the cake. Starting at one side, unroll the sugarpaste, allowing it to cover the cake loosely. With clean, dry hands, lightly smooth the sugarpaste over the top, excluding any trapped air bubbles. Ease gently on to the sides of the cake so that the excess sugarpaste is on the board.
4 Using a small knife, trim off the excess sugarpaste at the base of the cake. With your hands or a cake smoother, gently smooth the surface and side of the cake in circular movements to ensure a smooth and glossy finish. Leave to harden overnight.

To cover any shaped cake with sugarpaste

note

Ready-rolled sugarpaste icing is widely available (although in limited sizes and colours). Simply brush your marzipanned cake with some brandy or boiled and cooled water and ease the icing over the cake as detailed below.

Covering cake boards with sugarpaste

If you like the appearance of a cake board covered with sugarpaste, there are two ways to go about this.

- Brush the plain board with a little water, then cover with sugarpaste and leave it to dry. Place the marzipanned cake on the board, then apply the sugarpaste to the cake.
- Place the cake on the board. Roll out the sugarpaste large enough to cover the entire cake as well as the visible board and its sides. Lightly brush the cake and board with brandy or cooled boiled water. Place the sugarpaste over the cake and board, moulding it to fit around the cake, then trim around the board to neaten.

To ice with buttercream

Buttercream can be piped or spread on to cakes. Remember to fill your cake first, if needed, before icing. Always stir the buttercream well before spreading or piping to ensure that it has a smooth, soft consistency.

To pipe
Choose your nozzle and fill the piping bag with buttercream. After some practise, simply pipe on to your cake, squeezing with an even pressure. Allow to harden.

To spread
Use a palette knife to spread buttercream evenly over the top of your cake, paddling it backward and forward to eliminate any air bubbles. Have a jug of hot water near to dip the palette knife into as you spread the icing, so that it doesn't stick to the knife and pull up the crumb surface. Move the cake (on its cake board) to a turntable and use a palette knife to spread icing over the sides, paddling as you go. Use the palette knife to swirl the top and sides into a pattern. Leave to set.

To spread buttercream icing using a palette knife

To coat the side of your cake with nuts

Coating the sides of a cake with nuts adds flavour, crunch and visual appeal. Your cake needs to have been just iced with buttercream or frosting (so it is still sticky).

To coat
Put the iced cake on a large sheet of greaseproof paper. Working in sections, scatter nuts around the cake and use the paper to ease the nuts on to the cake – work slowly so that the nuts are not catapulted on to the top of the cake. Fill in any gaps by pressing the nuts on to the cake using your hands.

To ice with glacé icing

Glacé icing gives an even surface and is popular with children and adults alike. It takes a fair amount of time to dry so factor this in.

To glacé ice the top of a cake

Make a wide double thickness collar of greaseproof paper and wrap tightly around the cake, so that it is about 5cm (2 inches) above the top of the cake. Fix in place with a paper clip. Pour the icing on to the cake and spread almost to the collar. Leave to harden before removing the collar.

To glacé ice the top and sides of a cake

Simply pour the icing on to the centre of the cake and, using a palette knife, spread it right to the edges of the cake. Allow the icing to run down the sides evenly (with the help of your palette knife, if needed). Fill in any spaces with surplus icing from the bowl or from the baking sheet (taking care not to include crumbs). Clean the base.

To spread glacé icing on the top of a cake

To glacé ice over the top and sides of a cake

Food colourings

There has been quite a revolution in the food colouring industry over the past few years. Nearly gone are the watery liquids in a limited range of colours that dilute the mediums we were trying to colour, rather than tint them. These have been replaced with a range of vibrant pastes, powders and concentrated liquid colours and pens. Visit a specialist cake shop or website, as there are so many great products to help you create stunning cake designs.

Liquid colours

Liquid colours tend to be cheaper and more suitable for adding to cake mixes than to icing. Add drop by drop to achieve the desired colour – but care must be taken, as they can easily dilute the mixtures (and can cause mixes to curdle if too much is added). They are available in a wide range of everyday colours from most supermarkets.

Paste colours

These very concentrated moist pastes come in every possible colour you can need. They are ideal for colouring buttercream, sugarpaste and royal icing, as well as flower paste and marzipan. They are so concentrated that they will not affect the consistency of the mixture regardless of the depth of colour required. Apply with a cocktail stick a dot at a time until you have reached the desired colour. The pastes can also be applied neat with a paintbrush to add fine definition to work. When colouring with dark food colouring pastes, the colour can deepen on standing. Ideally (if using dark shades), tint to a shade lighter than the ultimate desired shade, then cover the icing/marzipan and leave to stand for 2–3 hours before using.

note

These are concentrated colourings, so approach with caution. You can always add more. If large quantities of coloured icing are required, always keep some of the coloured icing to match new batches. Ideally, match icing colours in daylight, not in artificial light.

Colour dusts

These edible powdered food colourings are suitable for kneading into sugarpaste, brushing to add colour to finished decorations, or for shading and colouring base icings on cakes. Dip a brush into the dust, then work the brush into or over the icing. A vast range of colours is available.

Lustre colours

These edible food colourings come in different powdered finishes – pearl, iridescent, metallic and sparkle. They give subtle colour with a high-sheen finish and are non-water soluble. The real advantage of these lustre colours is that they can be brushed on to dried decorations that have been made out of white sugar or flower paste. Different colours and shades may be applied to give a realistic effect.

Pollen dust

These tiny coloured granules are often used on flower centres instead of stamens to give a more realistic look. Brush the flower centres with a gum arabic glaze and dip into the chosen coloured pollen dust. Being edible, these dusts are better used on unwired flowers.

Glitter flakes

Made from paper-thin flakes of sugar, these edible decorations come in a range of colours and add instant sparkle to cakes. They need to be added to a sticky icing, or they'll just fall off, so use a gum arabic adhesive. Great sprinkled on to buttercream to give cakes or cupcakes a lift.

Edible glitter

Very fine-textured, edible glitter adds instant glamour to cakes and can also be used to highlight decorations. Sprinkle over sticky icing or brush sugarpaste with clear alcohol, then sprinkle away. You'll be amazed at the sparkle they give off. A wide range of colours and finishes (metallic, hologram, jewel, graphite, and so on) are available.

Pure gold or silver leaf

These are fine flakes or sheets of real gold and silver leaf. They look stunning when applied to cakes or decorations. An expensive decoration, this must be applied with care. If the surface is not sticky, then brush clear alcohol on to the surface and use fine tweezers or a paintbrush to apply the flakes. They look beautiful on chocolate.

Food colouring pens

These pens are filled with a variety of liquid food colourings. Their consistency can be a little unreliable when writing on to sugarpaste, royal icing or marzipan, but when used to add small colour accents to sugarcraft they can be useful.

tip

Try stencilling food colouring dusts on to the surface of a sugarpasted cake. Dampen a sponge or piece of muslin and wring out well. Scrunch it up and dab quickly into the food dust. Lightly dab the surface of the sugarpaste to imprint the colour. Re-dip into the colour as necessary. Always practise on an unwanted scrap of sugarpaste first to achieve the desired technique.

Piping

Piping is one of the most traditional skills, used to decorate all types of cakes. It takes practise to master, but the skill will come in useful frequently when decorating cakes.

The only equipment you need to start piping is a piping bag and a good set of nozzles. Make up a batch of royal icing and start practising by piping on boards, around cake tins and on to plates – that way you can reuse the icing time and again until you are competent. Try simple piping techniques first with basic nozzles, then as your skill and consistency improve, proceed to a larger selection of nozzles and techniques.

Making a paper icing bag

Reusable and disposable icing bags are widely available, but it's just as easy to make your own from greaseproof paper. Often delicate piping work is easiest achieved with a home-made icing bag, which can be snipped to a fine tip or used in conjunction with a piping nozzle. Once you've mastered the technique, make a batch of bags so that you have some ready and waiting. The bag can simply be disposed of once you have finished with it – just remember to rescue any piping nozzles first.

1 Cut out a rectangle of greaseproof paper measuring about 25.5 × 20.5cm (10 × 8 inches) – for smaller bags, cut a proportionally smaller rectangle. Fold in half diagonally, then cut along the crease. Use one of the triangles to continue.

2 Put the paper on the work surface with the apex of the triangle nearest to you. Bring the top left-hand point round to line up with the bottom point. Hold in place with your thumb and index finger.

3 Bring the right-hand point over and round the back, meeting at the bottom point. Pull together slightly to tighten the point. Fold over the points of the paper nearest to you to secure the bag.

4 To use, fill with icing and fold the paper over to seal. Snip the point off the bag (either straight across or at a slant), or fit with a metal nozzle before filling for more intricate designs.

Folding the paper into a triangle and then into an icing bag

Folding over the points of the paper to secure the bag

Filling a piping bag

1 If using a nozzle, snip off the tip of the piping bag and drop in a nozzle. If not using a nozzle, then leave the tip intact. If using a plastic piping bag, fold the top over to make a collar.

2 Hold the piping bag in your hand or stand it in a bowl or jug to support it. Fill half to two-thirds with icing. If using plastic, unfold the collar and twist to tighten to the level of the icing. Snip the tip if needed (either straight across or at a slant) and squeeze the bag gently to remove air bubbles and start the icing flowing. If using paper, fold over the open end until you hit the icing, then snip the tip if needed and squeeze the bag gently to remove air bubbles and start the icing flowing.

3 Never over-fill a piping bag, as it will become difficult to handle and as you squeeze, the icing will ooze out of the top. A good rule to remember is the smaller the piping nozzle, the smaller the piping bag and the less icing you require.

Piping techniques

To pipe well, it is essential to have your icing (be it buttercream, royal or whipped cream) at the correct consistency. When a wooden spoon is drawn out of the icing, it should form a fine but sharp point. If the icing is too stiff, it will be difficult to pipe; on the other hand, if it is too soft, the icing will run too freely, be difficult to control and lose definition. The larger the nozzle, the stiffer the icing needs to be; for a very fine writing nozzle, the consistency needs to be a little looser.

Piping designs

By varying the pressure, angle and nozzle shape and size you can produce many designs.

◆ To pipe lines

Fit a piping bag with either a plain or star nozzle – the smaller the hole, the finer the lines. Hold the piping bag at a 45-degree angle and 5mm (¼ inch) above the surface, then pipe towards you, securing the beginning of the line to the surface with a little pressure. Raise the bag slightly as the icing flows on to the surface in a straight or curved line. Press the piping bag to the surface lightly to secure the line, then pull away sharply to finish.

Filling a piping bag

Notes to remember when piping

- When piping cream, use only a small amount at a time, as over-handling in the piping bag can cause it to split and curdle, giving unsightly results. It is better to use larger nozzles to pipe cream.
- When piping, always keep your work area clean to avoid crumbs, dirt or blemishes appearing on your finished cake.
- Plan your pattern before piping and prick out a design with a pin to give you a template to follow (see page 63).
- Intricate designs are best piped on to silicone paper and left to dry, then fixed on to the cake with a dab of royal icing.
- Cover your bowl of icing with damp kitchen paper, clingfilm or a teatowel to prevent it from drying out.
- Always practise first – a board, cake tin or upturned plate all make good surfaces.

❷ To pipe beads or dots

The size of beads depends on the nozzle used and the pressure applied to the piping bag. Start with icing of a slightly softer consistency so that there are no sharp points on the ends of the beads. Hold the nozzle upright just above the surface, then squeeze out some icing on to the surface to make a bead (keeping the nozzle still). Pull up sharply to break the icing. Repeat the process to make a bead just next to the first one to make a chain. Smooth off the beads with a damp finger if you need to.

❸ To pipe rosettes/roses

Fit a piping bag with a star nozzle. Hold the piping bag straight above the surface, with the nozzle just touching the surface. Press out some icing to the size of the rosette you want, meanwhile lifting the bag slightly to give the rosette space. Stop pressing, then pull up sharply to break the icing. Repeat next to the first rosette to make a border.

❹ To pipe filigree

Fit a piping bag with a writing nozzle. Hold the piping bag with the nozzle like a pen, between thumb and forefinger. Pipe a thread of icing on to the surface of the cake to achieve the desired pattern. Keep the flow of the icing constant and work in all directions without breaking the thread for as long as possible. Re-join the icing where the break finished to keep the design constant.

❺ To pipe a shell

Fit a piping bag with a star nozzle. Hold the piping bag at a 45-degree angle and 5mm (¼ inch) above the surface. Pipe a small blob of icing and secure to the surface with a little pressure, then bring the bag slowly up, over the blob a little, then towards you and down again – almost like a rocking movement. Pull away sharply to finish off the shell. Pipe the next shell over the end of the previous one to make an edging.

❻ To pipe a rope/barrel

Fit a piping bag with a star nozzle. To pipe a rope, hold the piping bag at a 45-degree angle and 5mm (¼ inch) above the surface. Pipe a line in a continuous spiral motion. Alternatively, to make a barrel shape, gradually increase the pressure on the bag as you reach the middle of the line and then decrease the pressure towards the end.

❼ To pipe a lattice/trellis

Fit a piping bag with a fine, plain nozzle. Pipe parallel lines about 5mm (¼ inch) apart, keeping the lines as even as possible. Then over-pipe parallel lines (keeping the spacing the same) at 90-degrees to the initial rows of icing. A third layer of piping can be piped diagonally to the initial layers to create a more intricate finish.

❽ To pipe a scroll

Fit a piping bag with a star nozzle. Hold the piping bag at a 45-degree angle and 5mm (¼ inch) above the surface. Pipe the shape of a question mark (without the dot), then pull off sharply to break the icing. Repeat with another swirl (alternating directions, if you like).

❾ To pipe dropped-thread loop work

Fit a piping bag with a fine, plain nozzle. Pipe a thread of icing, securing the end to the side of the cake. Continue to pipe the icing just away from the side of the cake so that the thread forms a loop. Stop squeezing the piping bag when the loop is almost long enough, then press the thread of icing gently on to the side of the cake to secure the loop and break off the icing. Repeat the piping in this way until the loops go all the way round the cake. It is possible to repeat the procedure and to over-pipe each loop in the same or different colour icing, making sure you start your over-piped loop halfway across the first loop.

❿ To pipe basket weave

Pipe a plain vertical line from the top of the cake to the bottom. Fit another piping bag with a ribbon nozzle – this will produce a half plain, half fluted pipe. The finer the nozzle, the more intricate the finished weave will look. Starting at the top of the cake, pipe 2cm (¾ inch) long lines of icing horizontally across the vertical line at 1cm (½ inch) intervals. Now pipe another plain vertical line on the right-hand edge of the horizontal lines, then pipe 2cm (¾ inch) long horizontal lines, starting in between the first horizontal lines and going over the second vertical line. Repeat the process to give a basket weave.

⓫ To pipe leaves/leaf ropes

Fit a piping bag with a leaf nozzle. Hold the bag so that the point of the nozzle faces forward. Squeeze the bag hard to pipe the base of the leaf, then release so that the leaf trails off to a point. To make a leaf rope, pipe one leaf then start another leaf below it and continue so they are connected like a rope. Or pipe the leaves on alternate sides.

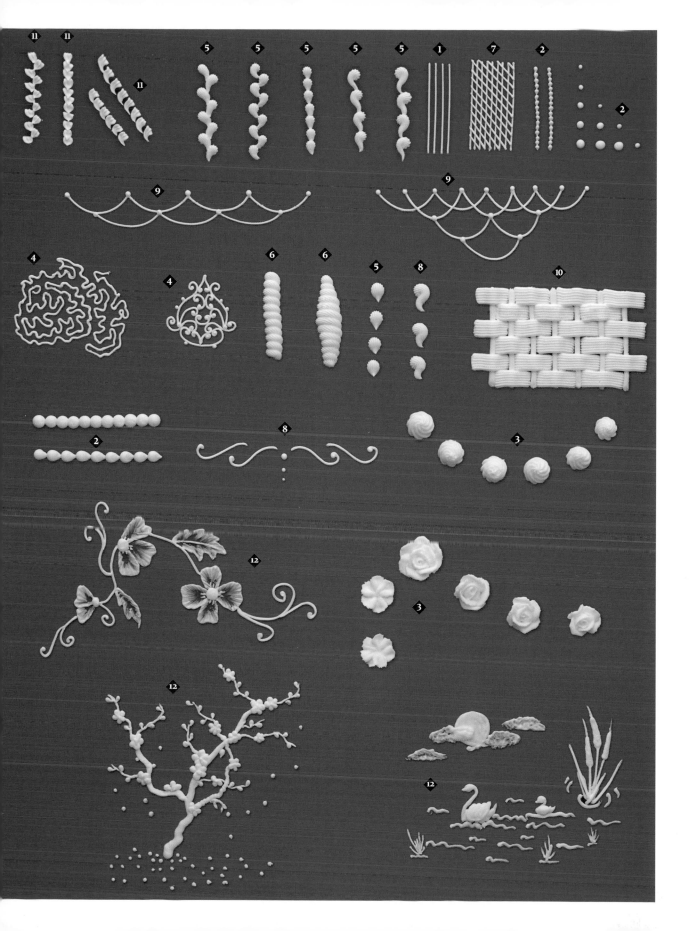

⌖ To pipe lace work

Often used in wedding cake decoration, lace piping is delicate work. Lace designs can be piped directly on to cakes or alternatively small sections can be piped on to non-stick paper, then left to dry before being fixed to the cake. When choosing your design, try to have lots of lines touching, as this makes the lace work stronger and will prevent breakages.

1 Draw your design on a piece of paper. Repeat the design several times, so that once you start piping you can continue. Put the design on a flat surface and cover it with a piece of run-on film, waxed paper or baking parchment. Secure the edges with tape or some icing.

2 Use run-out decoration consistency icing (see page 44) – with no glycerine added, so that the designs dry hard. Fit a small piping bag with a No. 0 plain nozzle, then quarter-fill the bag with icing and fold down the top.

3 With the nozzle held very closely to the surface, and under even pressure, pipe your design. Large pieces may be over-piped to give them double strength.

4 Pipe more pieces than required to allow for breakages. Leave the pieces to dry, then run a fine palette knife under them to release.

5 Attach the lace pieces to the cake with beads of royal icing. If the lace pieces need to be stored or transported, leave them on the run-on film or paper and pack them carefully, interleaved with tissue paper, into cardboard boxes.

Piping directly on to a cake

Use royal icing for intricate and delicate cake decorating work, as it sets hard and lasts for months. Lines and borders are best piped directly on to the cake, while more intricate shapes can be piped on to silicone paper, left to dry then, fixed on to the cake with a dab of royal icing. For lacework, draw your design on a paper template, then pipe on silicone paper laid over the top. Leave to dry completely before moving. Whole sheets of decorations can be piped on to silicone paper and stored like this in an airtight container for several weeks.

To pipe writing

Use fine, plain nozzles. Practise piping writing before attempting it on a cake. Work out how much space the letters take, and try to identify your style of handwriting (choose from different styles in cake decorating or calligraphy books). If you still feel unsure about piping freehand, then trace the word(s) on to greaseproof paper and, using a scribing needle or pin, mark the letters in the form of lots of tiny dots. Now simply pipe the letters by connecting the dots. Alternatively, write your message on to a dried sugar or flower-paste plaque and attach to the cake with a little water or royal icing.

Piping a scalloped design on to a cake

Making and using templates

To avoid mistakes and to ensure your design is symmetrical, it is best to make a template first.

1 Draw a pattern on greaseproof paper cut to the same size as the top or sides of the cake. If you are making a tiered wedding cake, remember you will need a proportionally sized template for each cake (and that only the edges of most of the tiers will be visible). To make a scalloped edge to a circle template, fold your template in half several times and use a compass (or the edge of a jar) to mark the curved edge, and then cut out this curve.

2 Attach the template to the surface or sides of your cake with a pin, then prick the surface with another pin or scribing needle, following the lines of your design.

3 Remove the paper and pipe over the pin marks.

Using a pin to prick a design on top of a cake

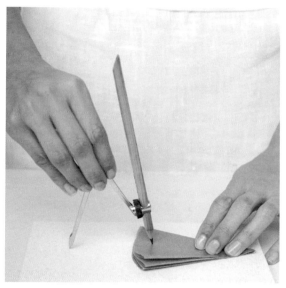

Using a compass to mark a curved edge

Attaching the template to the side of a cake with pins

Pricking the outline of the design using a scribing needle

Run-out designs

For these, flooding icing is used to fill shapes whose outlines have been piped with royal icing on to cakes, biscuits or templates. They can be made in any shape or form simply by tracing over a design or pattern. They are fragile and therefore it is wise to start with a small solid shape and progress from there.

To make flooding icing, thin down royal icing with a drop at a time of tepid water. Stir well after each addition until the desired consistency is reached (see piping consistency on page 44). Don't beat, just stir or you will add air bubbles to the design. When using different colours on one design, allow each one to dry before adding the next.

1 Fit a piping bag with a fine, plain nozzle. Place a drawing of your chosen design under a piece of run-out film (or waxed paper). Using royal icing thick enough for piping writing, pipe the outline of the design directly on to the run-out or waxed paper, following the drawing below it. Make sure that the outline of each section of the design is closed, so that the flooding icing doesn't leak when applied.

2 Fill another piping bag with the flooding icing (a nozzle isn't necessary), snip off the end and fill in the piped shapes, ensuring that the icing floods up to the edge of the outline. Fill so that the icing looks rounded, not flat, as it will shrink on drying. If needed, use a fine paintbrush to coax the icing into small areas. Burst any air bubbles with a pin.

3 Leave to dry completely (at least 24 hours). Pipe any details on to the run-outs at this stage and allow to dry again.

4 Using a fine palette knife, release the design from the film or paper and attach to the cake with a few beads of royal icing; alternatively, store on the film or paper, interleaved with tissue paper, in a cardboard box for a few months.

Using flooding icing to fill in the piped shapes

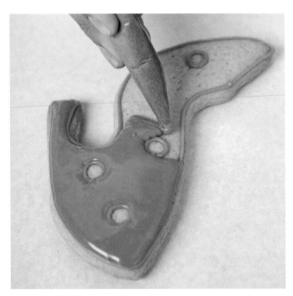

Flooding the design

Piping flowers and leaves

With the use of a petal nozzle and royal icing, many simple flower shapes can be piped. The nozzles come in a range of sizes, each suited to piping different size flowers. They are also available for left or right-handers. Colour the icing to your desired hue.

To pipe a basic flower

1 Fit a piping bag with a petal nozzle. Half-fill the bag with 'sharp peak' consistency royal icing (see page 44). Fold down the open end of the bag to seal. If you have one, use an icing nail (like a mini hand-held turntable, see page 17) with a small square of parchment paper on it, otherwise just use the paper.

2 Start by piping a petal – keep an even pressure and pipe a closed horseshoe shape (many modern icing nails will have dimensions of petals drawn on to them to help guide you). Slowly rotate the spinner (or manually rotate the paper if you don't have an icing nail) as you pipe the second petal.

3 By the time you pipe the third petal, two-thirds of the flower should be piped. If not, the petals are too fat or too thin. Keep rotating to pipe the remaining two petals. Pipe a contrasting bead of icing in the centre and leave to dry completely.

4 Remove the flower and attach to your cake with a bead of royal icing. Blush the blossoms with some colour or lustre dust, if you like (see page 57).

To pipe leaves

1 Make a small greaseproof piping bag (see page 58), fill with your desired leaf colour icing and cut the end of the piping bag into an inverted 'v'.

2 Put the tip of the piping bag directly on to the surface of the cake, or on some waxed paper. Press out icing to form a leaf shape. Repeat to make as many leaves as you want (or attach to make a border). Leave to dry on waxed paper. Remove and attach to your cake with a bead of royal icing.

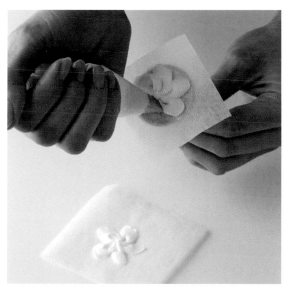

Piping a basic flower

Piping a leaf

To feather ice

Feathering is an easy technique that will create elegant results on cakes or cupcakes. It works best using glacé icing.

To feather ice 12 small cakes, you will need 225g (8oz) glacé icing (see page 56).

1 The top of the cupcakes need to be fairly flat for feathering to work. If they have risen, trim away the peak and dust away any crumbs with your fingers. Put the cakes on a flat surface.

2 Divide the icing into two. Now choose colours, but they need to contrast well for the feathering to stand out. Most classic is to leave the base colour white and dye the other bowl of icing with cocoa powder, or use a food colouring paste.

3 Cover six cakes with white icing and six with coloured icing, spooning on just enough to cover. Spread the icing to the edge of each cake with the help of a small palette knife or teaspoon.

4 Spoon the remaining icings into two separate small piping bags (without nozzles). Snip off the tips (finely) and, working quickly, pipe parallel lines 5mm (¼ inch) apart, or concentric circles, on top of the cakes in a contrasting colour.

5 Draw a cocktail stick or fine pointed knife through the piped icing in one direction and then in the opposite direction to create the feather pattern. Work quickly or the icing will form a skin and set before the pattern has been formed. Leave to set.

To feather ice

Piping – what went wrong

The most important thing when piping is to have the icing at the correct consistency. Unless otherwise stated, when a wooden spoon is drawn out of the royal, frosting or buttercream icing, it should form a fine but sharp point. Always remember, the larger the nozzle, the stiffer the icing needs to be. For a very fine nozzle, the consistency needs to be slightly softer.

The lines have broken
- The icing was too stiff
- The icing was pulled along rather than allowed to flow from the piping bag
- There were too many bubbles in the icing

The lines are wobbly
- The bag was squeezed too hard
- The icing was too runny

The lines are flat
The icing was too runny
The nozzle was held too near the surface of the icing

Icing and frosting cupcakes

The icing on cupcakes is now almost as important as the cake underneath. Icing helps keep the cake softer for longer (as long as the cakes are kept in their paper cases) and allows you to theme and decorate your cupcakes as desired.

Piping icing on to cupcakes

Many cupcake bakeries have developed a signature swirl of buttercream icing – practise and soon you'll have your own. Half-fill the piping bag with buttercream or frosting and hold the bag vertically as you pipe, squeezing gently from the top. Choose from the shapes below, or use your imagination.

Swirl

Fit a piping bag with a large star or plain nozzle. Starting from an outside edge, pipe an ever-decreasing circle on to the cupcake, slightly lifting the piping bag as you go. End with a point in the middle by sharply pulling away the piping bag.

Rosettes or blobs

The size of a rosette or blob depends on the nozzle used and the pressure applied to the piping bag. Fit the bag with a plain nozzle (to give blobs) or a star (to give rosettes). Holding the piping bag upright just above the surface, squeeze out some icing on to the cake (keeping the nozzle still). Pull up sharply to break the icing. Repeat the process to cover the cake surface with rosettes or blobs – it's easiest working in ever-decreasing circles. This method also looks good on the sides of a larger novelty or celebration cake.

Spreading

Start by gently brushing the top of the cooled cupcake with your finger or a brush to remove crumbs. Dollop a generous amount of buttercream or frosting on to the cake (it takes more than you might think) and gently spread the icing to the sides of the cake with a palette or butter knife for a smooth look. Alternatively, push the icing into a swirl or points with your spatula or knife.

Filling cupcakes

Before icing it, you can easily fill your cupcake with extra icing, buttercream or smooth jam. Fit a piping bag with a plain nozzle (not too fine), half-fill with the chosen filling and push the nozzle down through the top into the centre of the un-iced cake (alternatively hollow out some of the cake with a small knife first). Squeeze in some mixture, then ice as normal. It's worth cutting your first filled cake in half vertically to check how much filling you have managed to get into the cupcake.

Flooding cupcakes

Use a little less cake mixture when baking the cupcakes, so that when baked they don't quite reach the top of their cases. Spoon some glacé icing on top of the cooled cakes so that it floods out to the sides of the cases. Decorate with feathering (see opposite), sprinkles, dragees, gold leaf or other decorations as desired.

Covering with sugarpaste

Covering cupcakes with sugarpaste works best if the baked cupcakes are flat – if they have peaked during baking, then trim to flatten. Next, simply roll out some sugarpaste in the desired colour, to a thickness of 5mm (¼ inch). Measure the top of the cupcakes, then cut out circles of sugarpaste to match. Spread a thin layer of buttercream over the cupcake, then secure the sugarpaste circle in place.

If you don't want to completely cover the tops with sugarpaste, cut out smaller shapes of the sugarpaste – hearts always look nice. Leave to dry completely on baking parchment. Position on buttercreamed cupcakes (the decorations should be stiff enough to stand up).

note

For more decoration ideas see pages 71–147

Filling cupcakes

Ribbons

Ribbons are invaluable when decorating any type of celebration or everyday cake. They are the one non-edible decoration that transforms the simplest cake into something quite special.

There are, of course, many types of ribbon to choose from. If you are planning a very special cake, it is worth taking a trip to a haberdashery or specialist ribbon shop to find the ideal ribbon for the occasion.

The most popular ribbon is the double-faced polyester satin, which comes in a huge range of widths and colours. It is most useful for making bows, loops and tails for cake decorations and flower sprays. It is also used to band the edges of cake boards and to fit around the sides of cakes.

Ribbon bows

These are perfect for tying around the base of celebrations cakes, most notably Christmas cakes. Use a wide ribbon to create a big impact. Small bows, made with narrow ribbon, can be attached to the side or top of a celebration cake or cake board to enhance a border design or edging. Try making bows with long tail ends and curling them gently by pulling the ends over the cutting blade of a pair of scissors (hold one section of ribbon to the blade with your thumb, and pull it through, keeping the pressure tight). This technique looks pretty cascading over the edge of a cake.

Securing ribbons to cake boards

Choose a ribbon that's the same width as your cake board, then cut it to length. Wrap tightly around the sides of the board, then secure in place with a stainless steel pin.

Securing ribbons to the base of cakes

Choose your ribbon, then wrap it around the base of the cake and cut it so there is about a 1cm (½ inch) overlap. Secure one end of the ribbon in place with a stainless steel pin, then fold the edge of the other end to neaten it. Wrap the ribbon tightly around the cake and secure the folded edge in place over the other end with some pearl-topped pins (available from specialist cake shops, haberdasheries or via websites). Depending on the width of ribbon, you'll need one, two or three pins.

A selection of ribbons

Securing ribbons to the base of a cake

Ribbon insertion

Ribbon insertion is a simple but impressive way of decorating a cake covered with sugarpaste. Short lengths of ribbon are inserted at regular intervals into the surface of a cake freshly covered with sugarpaste, giving the illusion of a single piece of ribbon threaded through the icing. Different textures, widths and lengths of ribbon may be used to give this effect and, finished with bows or piping, make a stunning decoration.

1 Cut a strip of ribbon in the colour of your choice into sections of the desired length – if unsure, start with about 1cm (½ inch) strips.
2 Next, make a template. Take a strip of greaseproof paper and mark vertical pairs of slots, each to the depth of your ribbon and about 1cm (½ inch) apart (or just shorter than the length of your ribbon pieces), leaving a short space between the pairs. Or you can use a ribbon insertion tool.
3 Using pins, carefully fix the greaseproof paper to the sides of the cake. Then, using a small sharp knife (a scalpel is ideal), gently cut slots into the cake following the template marks.
4 Remove the paper and, using tweezers, a scalpel or a dedicated tool, insert one end of a ribbon piece into a slot. Bend the ribbon and push into the paired slot using the point of a knife or scalpel. Repeat around the cake.

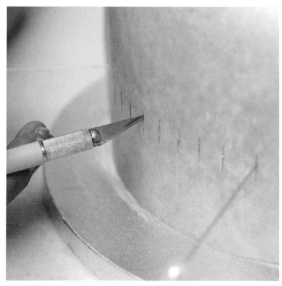

Cutting slots into the cake following the template marks

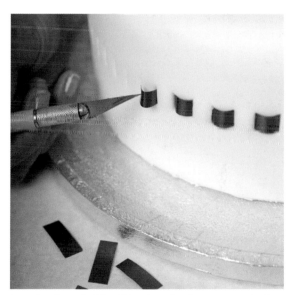

Inserting the end of the ribbon into the slot using a scalpel

Tiered and stacked cakes

If you are making a tiered cake, it is most important for the final result to choose the sizes of tiers carefully, avoiding a combination that would look too heavy. A basic, good proportion for a three-tier cake is 30.5cm (12 inches), 23cm (9 inches) and 15cm (6 inches). If in doubt, stack the empty cake tins on top of each other (base facing upwards) and this will give you a good idea of the finished proportions. Ideally, to give the cake balance, the depth of each tier should be the same. To ensure this, measure the depth of the uncooked mixture in the first cake tin. Take a note of this and ensure each subsequent cake mixture measures the same.

Using pillars to separate tiers

Pillars are the traditional method of separating tiers of cakes. They are available, round or square, in a variety of heights, colours and patterns and some can be fitted with dowels inside, which will support the weight of very heavy cakes.

To assemble a royal iced cake using pillars

It is easy to assemble a royal iced cake on cake pillars, as the solid pillars are placed directly on to the surface of the base cake, positioned accordingly and secured in place with a little royal icing before the next cake (which needs to be on a cake board) is placed on top.

Using a template: To be more accurate when assembling a square cake, cut out a paper template to the same size as the cake being supported above. Fold the template into four and place one pillar on the open corner of the template. Draw around the shape of the pillar and cut out. Open the template and place it on the centre of the base cake. Mark where the pillars need to go then remove the template. Repeat for the remaining tiers.

To use the template method for a round cake, fold the circular template of the supported cake into three, making a cone shape. Place one pillar on the edge of the broad end of the cone and draw around the shape. Cut out around the pillar shape. Open the template and place it on the centre of the base cake. Mark where the pillars need to be, then remove the template. Repeat for the remaining tiers.

To assemble a sugarpasted cake using pillars and dowels

If a sugarpasted cake is to be supported by pillars, acrylic or wooden skewers known as dowels must be inserted into the cake since the icing will not support the weight of the subsequent tiers. Pre-formed hollow cake pillars are then slipped over the dowels to conceal them and to support the cakes (which all need to be on cake boards). Arrange the hollow cake pillars on top of the cake until the position is right, then mark where the dowels should be. Use a paper template if required, as described above.

Insert a dowel into the centre of the positioned pillars and press vertically right through the icing into the cake until it is resting on the cake board. Continue inserting the dowels into the remaining pillars. Mark the dowels level with the top of each pillar. Carefully remove each pillar and dowel, and cut the dowels to the correct height following the marked lines. Replace the dowels and the pillars and position the cake. Repeat for the other tiers.

hint

If you need to deliver your cake, always assemble it at home so you are happy with its appearance. Dismantle the cakes, leaving the dowels in position, and pack the cakes into boxes. Pack the pillars separately. Reassemble at your destination.

Positioning the cake pillars on top of the cake

Using a template

Stacking a sugarpasted cake

Smaller cakes covered with sugarpaste may be placed directly on top of each other to produce a soft, rounded effect, and are simply supported by their cake boards. It looks like the cakes are directly stacked one on top of the other, but actually the cake boards (which should be the same diameter as the cakes) are taking the weight – and where larger cakes are concerned, so are the dowels.

Dowelling a stacked cake

1 Using a pin, mark the diameter of the middle cake on top of the base (largest) cake. Measure a square within the diameter and push a dowel vertically into each corner until it reaches the bottom of the cake and stands on the base cake board.

2 Using a pencil, mark on each dowel where it emerges from the surface of the cake. Remove the dowel.

3 Using a craft knife, cut the dowels at the mark, making sure they are all the same length. Push back into the holes and spread a little royal icing over the centre of the base cake.

4 Put the next cake layer on top, then repeat the previous steps. Top with the last layer and decorate as desired.

Stacking a tiered cake

Marking the diameter of the middle cake

Marking the dowel prior to cutting

Plastic or glass separators

Specialist cake shops or websites will sell plastic or glass cake separators – which are usually cubes or tubes. These are used instead of pillars and add a modern touch to a celebration cake. They can be filled with flowers, petals, crystals, pearls, coloured glass pebbles or foam beads, which can all be matched to the theme of the celebrations. Dowels will need to be added to support the corners of each separator.

Filling a plastic cake separator with floral berry foam beads

Cake Decorating

Full-blown cake decorating can be time-consuming, but there are some quicker alternatives. Here are some useful ideas that work well on both individual cakes and larger novelty or celebration cakes.

Quick decoration ideas

- Sprinkle desiccated coconut, sugar sprinkles, grated chocolate or coloured sugar over frosted or buttercreamed cakes. Make your own coloured sugar by massaging a small amount of food colour into some granulated sugar in a polythene bag. Leave to dry before use.
- Top cakes with whipped cream, berries and a dusting of icing sugar.
- Decorate with sweets – jelly tots, chocolate buttons, Smarties, liquorice allsorts, crushed boiled sweets and Maltesers all work well.
- Freeze-dried petals make stunning decorations. Buy in specialist cake shops or via websites and make sure they are the edible variety.
- Fresh flowers make a simple and beautiful decoration for individual or plain iced celebration cakes. In singles or clusters, gerbera, primroses, violets and roses work particularly well. Ensure your flowers have not been sprayed with chemicals, as they will be in contact with edible material.
- On small cakes, a single crystallised flower (see page 87), violet or rose petal makes a stunning decoration.

- Why not add two colours of icing to your piping bag to give a multi-coloured swirl.
- Ready-made sugar or wafer flowers are available from all good cake shops or via websites. Simply fix on to your cake with some royal icing.
- Look in the baking aisle of the supermarket for ready-made decorations.
- Make small decorations out of sugarpaste or marzipan – such as baby booties, ladybirds or hedgehogs. Leave to dry, then press into freshly iced cupcakes.
- Cut template shapes (such as stars or hearts) out of greaseproof paper. Place over cupcakes and dust with icing sugar, then remove the template. Or use a section of a doily for a ready-made design.
- Edible glitter, available in specialist cake shops or via websites, adds a striking finish to cakes and cupcakes. Simply sprinkle some on to wet icing (buttercream, frosting or royal icing), or brush dried sugarpaste with clear alcohol, then sprinkle away.
- Bows and ribbons add instant glamour.

Modelling with sugarpaste

Sugarpaste can be moulded or rolled thinly and dries without cracking, which make it a good modelling material. Fully dried decorations will keep indefinitely if packed carefully in an airtight container – use bubble wrap or tissue paper to prevent breakages.

Sugarpaste can be bought in a variety of colours – or home-made sugarpaste can be easily dyed to the colour you want. If dyeing, add minute amounts of food colouring (pastes are ideal) with the tip of a cocktail stick and knead in before adding any more.

Before using sugarpaste for modelling, always knead it well first to help it soften and smooth.

When modelling with sugarpaste, always have some hard white vegetable fat to hand – a little smeared on the surface of your fingers will stop sugarpaste sticking without the paste drying out. As always when using sugarpaste, wrap any that you are not using in clingfilm to stop it drying out.

Edible glue

Widely available from all specialist cake shops or via websites, edible glue is suitable for all sugarcraft purposes – especially when modelling figures and making flowers.

Gum tragacanth

Available from specialist cake shops or via websites, gum tragacanth is a natural gum that strengthens many types of icing. Just a little of it kneaded into sugarpaste (follow the directions on the pot) will make the sugarpaste easier to handle – it will roll thinner without tearing, model without cracking and dry faster and more firmly. Once the gum has been added, wrap the sugarpaste well in clingfilm and let it rest for at least an hour before using. A very worthwhile investment. When sugarpaste has gum tragacanth added to it, you can also achieve very delicate modelling work, which would normally require expensive flower paste.

Modelling flowers

Once the realm of experts only, sugar flowers had to be moulded entirely by hand. Luckily, there are now flower, petal and leaf cutters for almost every variety of flower, which give lifelike results. These tools certainly make flower modelling more time-efficient (and easier), but there's still charm to those moulded by hand. Always try to have a picture of the real flower in front of you when making sugar flowers – this is the best way to make your flower as lifelike as possible.

To make blossom plunger cutter flowers

1 Buy or colour sugarpaste to your desired shade. Using an acrylic rolling pin, roll out some sugarpaste very thinly so that you can almost see through it.
2 Using a small, medium or large plunger blossom cutter, cut out blossom shapes. Eject the flower (by pressing the plunger) onto a piece of foam pad, then press the centre of the blossom with a round bone tool (or your little finger) to bend it slightly inwards.
3 If the blossoms are going to have stamens in the centre, make a pinhole in the centre of each as it is made. Leave to dry.

4 Brush the back of the blossoms with a little blob of edible glue, then thread a stamen through (making sure the head nestles in the cup of the blossom).

Pressing a blossom plunger cutter flower

Wiring plunger blossoms into sprays

To wire plunger blossoms into sprays

Use this technique to bind together any wired flowers. Blossom sprays are particularly useful for filling in more complicated flower sprays and arrangements.

For wiring plunger blossoms you will need about a 10cm (4 inch) length of 28–30 gauge florist's wire and tape. It looks more realistic to make up the sprays with different-sized blossoms.

1 Make a small hook at one end of the wire. Put a stamen (attached to a blossom) through the loop and squeeze together to secure. Attach the florist's tape as close to the base of the blossom as possible, then twist the wire in your fingers (spiralling down the tape as you do so), to cover about 1cm (½ inch) of the wire and stamen with the tape.
2 Hold another blossom flush against the wire and continue to tightly wrap the tape around the stems to join the blossoms securely to the wire. When you have added as many blossoms as you want, continue to wrap the tape around the remaining wire stem to neaten.
3 Make as many assorted flower sprays as needed. Store, interleaved with tissue paper, in a cardboard box in a cool, dry place.

To make a rose

You'll see many techniques for making moulded sugar roses, but it's about finding the method that suits you. The one detailed here is readily achievable and does not require specialist petal cutters.

1 Buy or colour sugarpaste to your desired shade. Make a cone of sugarpaste, which will form the centre of the rose, as well as the base for it to stand on while modelling. Take a pea-sized amount of your sugarpaste and shape into a petal in your palm, making it thicker at the base and finer at the rounded top edge. Wrap the first petal, thicker-part down, around the top part of your cone to make the rose bud – the lower part of the cone holds the rose while modelling but will later be cut off.

2 Make another petal as before, then position it so that the centre of the second petal overlaps the join of the first one. Press one side on to the bud and leave the other slightly lifted off. Now make a third petal – slightly larger than the first two. Attach this petal by tucking it inside the lifted part of the second petal. Press gently around the bud at the base and bend the petals over a little at the top to give them movement.

3 Continue working around the rose as above. When the rose is the desired size, cut the rose at the base of the petals and place on a piece of foam pad to dry for at least 24–48 hours.

4 When dry, brush with lustres, if you like, and attach to your cake with a small dab of royal icing.

tip

If you want to make a rose bud, then simply attach fewer petals and keep the tops of the petals tighter.

To cut out leaves

Buy or colour sugarpaste to your desired shade of green (alternatively, you can use white sugarpaste and later brush with a green food colouring dust). Lightly dust the work surface with sifted icing sugar or cornflour, then roll out the sugarpaste thinly and stamp out shapes with a leaf cutter (plunge cutters are ideal for this, as they will imprint veins on to the leaf). If you don't have a leaf cutter, then use a small knife and imprint the veins manually.

Allow the leaves to dry flat on some baking parchment, or bend them over a piece of dowel or crumpled foil to give them movement.

To make a daisy

Roll out some light pink, yellow or white sugarpaste into small rectangles. Make a line of cuts or snips along one long edge of each rectangle. Open out the snips to fan them and flatten very lightly. Brush the un-snipped edge of the rectangle with some water and roll up the wet edge. Fan out the petals and lightly squeeze the unsnipped base to make sure it is secure. Press a small yellow ball of sugarpaste into the centre of the petals to represent the stigma of the daisy, and attach a sturdy green sugarpaste stalk to the base of the flower if you like. Leave to dry before using.

Cutting the rose from its base

Cutting along the edge of a sugarpaste rectangle

Moulding animals

Let your imagination run wild – it will help you to create fabulous real and mythical creatures. Use a little water or edible glue to stick the pieces together.

To make a mouse

1 Roll some white sugarpaste into a pear shape for the body. Roll two small balls and flatten for the ears. Using scissors or a cocktail stick, snip or press whiskers into the icing.
2 Roll two small balls of pink sugarpaste and flatten them. Attach to the white ears with a little water or edible glue. Pinch the base of the ears together and press into the mouse at either side of the head (use a cocktail stick to help you).
3 Roll a length of sugarpaste into a tail and attach to the mouse with a little water or edible glue. Pipe on the eyes.

To make a duck

1 Take a marble-size piece of yellow sugarpaste and roll it into a ball. Flatten slightly between thumb and forefinger to make the head.
2 Using some more yellow sugarpaste, mould a larger pear shape to make the body. Pinch the tapered end upwards to make the duck's tail.
3 If you like, using a pair of scissors, snip both sides of the duck (with the tip of the scissors facing the head) and pinch the cuts out to make wings.
4 Take a tiny amount of orange sugarpaste and mould into a beak with a rounded, rather than pointy, end. Attach to the head, then pipe on the eyes.

Attaching the tail to a sugarpaste mouse

Piping the eyes on a sugarpaste duck

Sugarpaste penguins

Hedgehog, ladybirds and tortoise cake buns

To make a penguin

1 Take a piece of black sugarpaste and roll it into an egg shape. Roll a small piece of white sugarpaste into a ball and flatten into an oval. Stick the oval to the front of the penguin's body.

2 Roll a small piece of black sugarpaste into a ball and place on top of the body to make the head. Using a cocktail stick, make two small holes for the eyes. Shape a small piece of orange sugarpaste into a cone shape and press gently on to the head to form a beak.

3 Squeezing small bits of black sugarpaste between your fingers will give you wing shapes – attach these to the body. Using the orange icing, make two small flattish ovals and attach to the base of the body to make the feet.

4 To make a scarf, roll out a piece of contrasting-coloured icing, cut into a long strip and wrap around the penguin's neck. To make a hat, mould a cone and attach to the penguin's head. Leave to dry completely.

5 Attach to cakes or cupcakes with some buttercream or royal icing.

To make a ladybird cake

1 Roll out red sugarpaste thinly and cover cold cake buns.

2 Using black writing icing, pipe wings, spots and a smile on the ladybirds and use chocolate drops for eyes.

To make a tortoise cake

1 Roll out green sugarpaste thinly and cover cold cake buns.

2 Use brown writing icing to draw 'shell' markings and add white chocolate drops.

3 Make the heads, legs and tails from brown icing, and attach to the body with a little jam.

4 Add silver balls for eyes.

To make a hedgehog cake

1 Cover buns with chocolate butter-cream, shaping to form a snout.

2 Decorate with chocolate sprinkles, silver or gold balls for eyes and a dolly mixture sweet for the nose.

Making Christmas decorations with sugarpaste

Christmas can make even the most terrified sugarcrafter try their hand at this skill. Here are a few easy ideas to get you started.

Dust your work surface with sifted icing sugar or cornflour to stop the sugarpaste from sticking, then, using an acrylic rolling pin, roll out sugarpaste to a 3mm (1¹/8 inch) thickness. Using Christmas cookie cutters (such as stars, bells, trees, reindeers, and so on), stamp out shapes and brush the underside with water. Position on your sugarpasted cake and gently press into place. Alternatively, leave the shapes to dry on a sheet of baking parchment, then rest them on the sides and top of the cake.

Christmas stars

Christmas roses

Christmas snowman

Christmas holly

Christmas snowman

1   Shape three ever-decreasing balls of white sugarpaste. Fix the middle ball on top of the largest ball with a little edible glue, to make a body. Now glue the smallest ball to the body to make the head.

2   Using tiny beads of black sugarpaste, make three 'coal' buttons and fix down the middle of the centre white ball. Now fix two black beads in place for the eyes, and more to make a smile (spacing the beads a little way apart to resemble coal).

3   Using some coloured sugarpaste (red or green are particularly Christmassy), shape a cone for the snowman's hat and a strip for the scarf. Stick two small twigs or cocktail sticks into the central white ball to make the arms Leave to dry before using.

Christmas roses

1   Dust your work surface with sifted icing sugar or cornflour. Roll out some white sugarpaste. Using a plain cocktail cutter or the base of an icing nozzle, cut out small rounds. Mould each round into a petal shape, pinching one end to a point.

2   Arrange five petals in an overlapping circle and secure in position with a little royal icing or some pressure. Gently twist the petals to give them movement.

3   Next, dye some royal icing bright yellow. Pipe a large bead into the centre of each flower. Next, pipe small dots around the central bead, lifting the piping bag at the same time to form the stamens. Leave to dry before using.

tip

Using a cutter, stamp out white sugarpaste holly leaves, then mark the leaves with a cocktail stick to show the veining. Dry the leaves twisted gently over the handle of a wooden spoon for 24 hours. Paint the holly leaves with gold edible glitter and arrange as a border around your cake.

Christmas Tree Cake

Cuts into about 40 portions

icing sugar, sifted, to dust

about 1kg (2¼lb) white sugarpaste
(ideally strengthened with gum tragacanth,
see page 75)

blue food colouring

1 × 20.5cm (8 inch) round fruit cake, top-iced
only with marzipan and sugarpaste

225g (8oz) glacé icing (see page 56) – a little
thicker than normal

You will also need:
a set of 6 or 7 nesting star cutters

Per serving
383 cals; 9.1g fat (of which 4g saturates);
77g carbohydrate; 0.2g salt

An easy cake decoration with stunning end results.

1 Line some baking sheets with baking parchment. Lightly dust a worksurface with icing sugar, then roll out half the sugarpaste until it is about 1cm (½ inch) thick. Cut out stars – you need to end up with two stars of each size. Reroll the trimmings and use more sugarpaste as needed. Leave the stars to dry on the baking sheets. Cut out two extra small stars and make a cut to the middle of one of the stars (large enough to later slot the other small star into). Dry flat.

2 Reroll the remaining sugarpaste and choose a star size that fits nicely around the sides of the cake. Cut out enough stars to make a border around the cake. Leave to dry – keeping them away from the first batch of stars to avoid confusion.

3 Dye any remaining sugarpaste pale blue and shape into rough 2cm (¾ inch) cubes – these will become the presents around the tree.

4 Put the cake on to a cake board, if it is not on one already. Stack the dried tree stars in a pyramid in the centre of the cake – starting with the two biggest stars first and securing to the cake/each other with a little glacé icing. Continue stacking (trying not to align the points) until you have only 2 small star remaining – one plain and one slotted. Slot one star into the other and position vertically on top of the tree, securing in place with icing (or use just one star, if you prefer).

5 Stick the cake stars around the side of the cake, securing in place with glacé icing. Dye any remaining glacé icing pale blue and check the consistency is good for piping. Transfer to a piping bag fitted with a small plain nozzle and pipe icicles around the top edge of the cake (you may need to make a little more icing, depending on how much you have used as glue).

6 Position the presents around the tree and pipe on ribbon and bows with the remaining glacé icing. Leave to dry.

Sugarpaste shapes

Rolling and stamping out shapes from sugarpaste is a relatively easy way to create dramatic finishes for your cake. Simply roll out sugarpaste thinly on a surface lightly dusted with sifted icing sugar or cornflour. Cut out small icing shapes using cutters (or freehand), then either stick immediately on to cakes or allow to dry first before applying.

Using a template to cut out shapes

1 Trace your design on to greaseproof paper, ideally dividing it into sections for ease of use.
2 Select the colours for the chosen design; alternatively, cut out the design in white sugarpaste and paint the pieces with food colours when the design has dried.
3 Dust your work surface with sifted icing sugar or cornflour to stop the sugarpaste from sticking, then, using an acrylic rolling pin, start rolling out your first colour of sugarpaste thinly. Put the template on top of the sugarpaste and, using a scribing needle or pin, mark the outline of the relevant shape.
4 Using a small sharp knife or scalpel, cut out the design pieces and continue using the various coloured sugarpaste and template until all the elements have been cut out.
5 Assemble the pieces to make sure they fit, then apply them piece by piece on to the iced cake – take care not to over-handle or mis-shape the pieces. Secure the design to the cake using a little egg white or edible glue. Alternatively, allow the pieces to dry (in the correct shape) on a sheet of baking parchment before fixing to your cake.

Crimping sugarpaste

This technique is quick and easy to master – as long as you have a crimping tool (widely available in specialist cake shops or online). These tweezer-shaped tools come with different end pieces, which produce curved lines, scallops, ovals, diamonds and hearts, to name but a few. To obtain the best results, always practise first on a spare piece of sugarpaste.

1 Cover a cake with sugarpaste, but do not leave it to dry. Dust the crimper lightly with sifted icing sugar or cornflour to prevent it sticking.
2 Hold the crimper like a pencil and place, slightly opened, on to the edge of the cake. Lightly press into the cake and squeeze to mark the pattern on to the sugarpaste.
3 Gently release the crimper and lift off, taking care that it does not spring apart or it will tear and ruin the pattern.
4 Place the crimper next to the marked pattern and repeat around the cake, dusting the crimper occasionally to stop it sticking.

Using a template to cut out shapes

Crimping sugarpaste

To make sugarpaste frills

Layers of fine sugarpaste frills cascading down the sides of a cake can look absolutely spectacular. They can be attached as a single layer or in many more layers in scalloped or arched designs. Ideally, use sugarpaste strengthened with gum tragacanth (see page 75).

1 Dust your work surface with sifted icing sugar or cornflour to stop the sugarpaste from sticking, then, using an acrylic rolling pin, roll out one piece of sugarpaste thinly.

2 Cut out the desired shape – dedicated circular frill cutters are best, but alternatively try a plain or scalloped narrow strip – and place on a flat surface. Dip a cocktail stick into some icing sugar or cornflour, place it on the edge of the sugarpaste shape and roll the stick backwards and forwards along a short section of the shape until the edge begins to frill. Move over the edge of the sugarpaste until it is all frilled.

3 If using a circular frill cutter, slice the frill open with a knife and ease it to the shape of your cake. Attach to the cake with some royal icing. Apply some coloured or lustre dust to your frills, if you like.

To make sugarpaste frills

To make cut-out extension pieces

Extension sugar pieces may be made from cutting out shapes of sugarpaste and leaving them to dry, then attaching them to the cake, to stick out beyond the sides or edges.

Using sugarpaste would be fine, but for extra strength and quick-drying properties use a mixture of 50% sugarpaste and 50% flower paste (or sugarpaste strengthened with gum tragacanth, see page 75).

1 Roll out the sugarpaste (mixture) so thinly that you can almost see through it.

2 Using cutters of varying shapes and sizes, or a template, cut out one or two pieces from the rolled-out icing. Cut out any necessary details.

3 Arrange the pieces on a flat surface dusted with cornflour or on a piece of foam pad and leave in a warm, dry place until hard. Repeat this procedure to make the number of extensions needed to decorate the cake. Always make a few extra pieces to allow for breakages.

4 When the pieces are dry, tint with coloured dust if you like, or paint with food colouring pastes. Now arrange the pieces (without glueing) on the cake to ensure they fit.

5 Attach the sugar pieces with royal icing and allow to dry overnight.

Edible photographs

For an unusual effect, personal photographs can be printed on to edible wafer paper or directly on to icing and fixed to the cake. Printer-friendly wafer paper and edible ink cartridges can be obtained from specialist websites or you can place an order with a company who will do the printing for you. Your sheet will be sent to you with instructions on how to fix it to your cake.

Modelling with flower paste

Sugar flower paste is a modelling material that's ideal for making intricate, ultra-fine decorations like flowers, leaves, bows and frills, as well as intricate plaques to rest on cakes (plaque cutters of varying shapes and sizes are sold in specialist cake shops or via websites). Flower paste is easy (almost elastic) to handle and sets incredibly hard without becoming too brittle – in its dried state it is often mistaken for porcelain.

Flower paste can be bought in small sachets or tubs from cake specialist shops or via websites, but it is fairly expensive. Alternatively, you can have a go at making your own – liquid glucose and gum tragacanth are available from all cake icing and decorating specialists.

When modelling larger flowers or plaques, another option is to mix flower paste in a 50:50 ratio with sugarpaste to make a quick-drying medium that still has many of the benefits of flower paste.

Makes 350g (12oz) flower paste

225g (8oz) icing sugar
1 tbsp gum tragacanth
1 rounded tsp liquid glucose
1–2 tbsp cold water

1 Sift the icing sugar and gum tragacanth into a bowl. Make a well in the centre and add the liquid glucose and 1 tbsp water. Mix together with your finger to form a soft paste, adding a touch more water as necessary. Knead on a work surface dusted lightly with sifted icing sugar until smooth, white and free from cracks.

2 Put into a polythene bag or wrap in clingfilm to exclude air. Leave to rest for 2 hours before use, then re-knead. Use small pieces at a time, making sure the remaining flower paste is tightly wrapped to stop it drying out.

hint

If you can't find flower paste and have no time to make it, use sugarpaste strengthened with gum tragacanth (see page 75).

tip

Only use liquid or powder food colouring to colour flower paste or else it will not dry properly.

To make a flower paste daisy

1 Lightly dust the work surface with sifted icing sugar. Using an acrylic rolling pin, roll out some white flower paste thinly, using a little white fat if necessary to stop it sticking. Using a daisy cutter, cut out the shape. Use a modelling knife or scalpel to cut each petal in half to double the number of petals (make sure the daisy is not sticking to the surface).

2 Using a cocktail stick, lightly roll the tip of each petal on a flat surface, to frill it slightly, then put on to a piece of foam pad and press the centre of each with a round bone tool (or your little finger) to bend it slightly inwards.

3 Make a small hook in the end of a short length of 26-gauge florist's wire. Dip the hook end in edible glue, then cover the hook with a small bead of yellow flower paste. If you want, repaint the beads with glue and dip into pollen dust. Push the wire through the daisy so that the centre nestles into the inward bend of the daisy. Brush the underside with edible glue to secure.

4 Using the cutter provided, cut out the calyx (the fine greenish petals at the base of the flower) from thinly rolled green flower paste, or shape using your fingers. Thread on to the back of the daisy and secure with some more edible glue. Leave the daisy to dry on a piece of foam pad (pricking the wire into the foam so that the daisy doesn't bend).

5 To make the flower ever more special, brush the base of the petals with moss green coloured dust. If you want, combine the daisies into sprays, following the method described on page 75.

Frilling the petals of a flower paste daisy

Moulding figures

Moulding figures requires care and patience. They need two key factors to make them come alive. One is the proportion and the other is facial expression. With practise, you'll learn the feel of the moulding material and how much pressure to apply.

Use sugarpaste (ideally strengthened with gum tragacanth – see page 75) or marzipan for figure modelling. Most figures are made from three basic shapes: a ball for the head, a sausage for the body, and pears for the limbs. Body parts are often moulded separately, left to dry and then assembled. Always gauge the size of your figures in relation to the cake and factor in the drying time.

Marzipan is used for figures that need to be sturdy and stand upright.

It is firm and easy to work with, although the texture is slightly grainy in comparison to sugarpaste. Make sure you allow at least 24 hours drying time for marzipan figures so that the oil in the mixture will not soak into the iced cake. Sugarpaste is used for delicate figures and finer work. It can be made wafer thin without cracking and dries solid (after many days).

Modelling tools are available to shape and mark patterns; however, there will be lots of kitchen utensils in your drawers that will do similar jobs – wooden skewers, small spatulas and small sharp knives are all useful. It's a good idea to invest in a fine brush for painting features using food colouring pastes. If applying colourings directly on to models, ensure the figures are dry first.

To make a wrestler

1 Roll a ball of flesh-coloured sugarpaste or marzipan for the head. Roll a long sausage of the same colour for the arms. Use your little finger to mark muscle definition and flatten each end to make hands. Add finger definition with a knife or cocktail stick. Roll out two flesh-coloured sturdy legs, marking the muscles.

2 Shape some contrasting-coloured marzipan or sugarpaste into the trunk of the body, making it 'v' shaped where the legs will join.

3 Make two boots: they need to match the width of the base of the legs where they will join, and be quite solid and flat so that the figure will stand.

4 Firmly press the arms to the top of the body. Cut the top of the legs at an angle and press to the base of the body (on the sides of the 'v'). Press the boots on to the base of the legs. Put on to baking parchment to dry (lying down).

5 When dry, thinly roll out some more coloured marzipan or sugarpaste and cut strips for the straps of the wrestler suit. Position over the shoulders. Using food colouring pastes, paint in the eyes and a mouth. Shape a little brown or yellow marzipan or sugarpaste to make the hair and moustache. Attach to the head.

Moulding the body parts for the wrestler

The finished wrestler

Modelling with marzipan

Marzipan can be used to model decorations such as flowers, fruit and figurines. These modelled shapes are ideal for adding interest to birthday, novelty or individual cakes.

As marzipan generally only comes in white or yellow, it often needs to be coloured. To colour the marzipan, dip the tip of a cocktail stick into the desired shade of food colouring paste, then smear it on to the marzipan. Start with a little first, as you can always add more. Knead together until the desired shade is achieved (you might need to dust your hands with icing sugar to stop any sticking).

When you have the desired shade, knead a small amount until soft and pliable, then roll or mould into shapes. Make sure you factor in at least 24 hours drying time for marzipan shapes, so that the oil in the mixture will not soak into the iced cake.

To make marzipan carrots

1   Knead 65g (2½oz) marzipan until pliable. Add a dab of orange food colouring paste and knead evenly until distributed. Divide into 15 evenly sized pieces and roll each into a small cone. Put the cones on a tray lined with baking parchment.
2   Mark ridges down the top and sides of each cone to give the carrot life. Use a small amount of green marzipan or chopped angelica to make the top of the carrot. Leave to dry before using.

To make marzipan fruit

Lemon Colour some marzipan yellow and mould into a plump oval. Roll it over the fine surface of a grater to give the lemon peel some texture. Press in a clove at one end to make the stalk, if you like, or use some brown marzipan. Colour a little marzipan green and shape into a leaf.

Orange Colour some marzipan orange and roll into balls. Using a cocktail stick, mark the skin to give texture. Add green marzipan leaves.

Pineapple Colour some marzipan yellow and roll into a plump oval. Mark a criss-cross pattern. Colour some marzipan green. Shape a small rectangle and snip along one edge. Carefully round the snips (without tearing them off the base) to make the pineapple top. Attach to the pineapple base.

Strawberry Colour some marzipan red and shape into a rounded cone. Roll it over the medium-coarse surface of a grater. Colour a little marzipan green and shape to form the hull (or use a suitably-shaped plunger cutter).

Grapes Colour some marzipan pale green and some mauve. Shape the green into a cone and flatten slightly. Roll small balls of mauve marzipan for grapes and stick to the flattened cone. Add a green vine leaf.

Apple Colour some marzipan pale green and roll into a ball. Press a clove into the top, or use some brown marzipan.

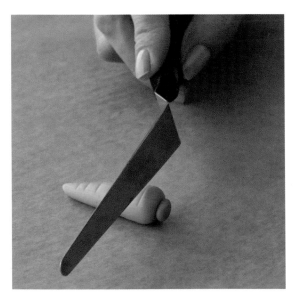

To make marzipan carrots

Marzipan fruit

Crystallising flowers, petals, leaves and herbs

Edible flowers, petals and leaves can easily be crystallised at home to make stunning individual decorations for cupcakes, or clustered together on a celebration cake. Rose petals and buds, daisies, pansies, violas, lavender sprigs and leaves are all suitable. Small fruit such as grapes, redcurrants and physalis can also be crystallised. Before crystallising, always ensure you use flowers and leaves that have not been sprayed with chemicals.

For best results, use flowers with a small number of petals, such as violets, primroses, rose petals or fruit blossoms – apple, pear or cherry. Choose flowers or petals that are fresh and free from damage, bruises or blemishes. These are best picked in the morning once the dew has lifted and the flowers are completely dry.

Herb leaves can also be crystallised – mint is the most popular because of its flavour. Be just as selective when choosing leaves – they need to be fresh and blemish free.

There are two methods of crystallising. The first is simpler, and involves painting the flowers, petals or leaves with egg white, then sprinkling with caster sugar and leaving them to dry. Items crystallised with egg white can generally be kept for one to two months. The second method involves painting the flowers, petals or leaves with gum arabic, then waiting for it to be absorbed before sprinkling with caster sugar and leaving to dry. Any crystallised item will be very delicate, so handle and store carefully in a cardboard box for up to several months.

Gum arabic

Gum arabic is available from specialist cake shops or websites. It is a powder that can be used to make an edible glaze, adhesive or thickener.

Crystallising using egg white

1 egg white

edible flowers, petals, or herb

caster sugar

The simplest method of crystallisation uses egg white – just remember to factor in drying time.

1   Whisk the egg white lightly in a small bowl until frothy (but not in any way stiff). Using a small paintbrush, paint both sides of the dry flower, petal, herb or fruit with a thin layer of egg white (do not dip straight into the egg white or the layer will be too thick). Sprinkle both sides with caster sugar.
2   Shake off surplus sugar and leave to dry on a baking sheet lined with parchment paper for about two days in a warm, dry place. If necessary, sprinkle a second time with sugar to ensure an even sugar coating. Leave to dry in a warm place until solid. Store in a cardboard box lined with kitchen paper for one to two months.

Crystallising using gum arabic

1 tbsp gum arabic

2 tbsp rose water

caster sugar

rose petals

Crystallising with gum arabic gives longer-lasting results.

1   Put the gum arabic and rose water into a small, clean screw-top jar and shake together for 2–3 minutes. Leave for 1–3 hours until the gum arabic has dissolved.
2   Paint both sides of the dry flower, petal or herb with the gum mixture (do not dip straight into the gum mixture or the layer will be too thick). Put on to baking parchment and leave for about 24 hours or until the solution has been absorbed.
3   Sprinkle both sides of the petals with caster sugar and shake off any surplus. Sprinkle with sugar a second time until evenly coated. Leave to dry on a baking sheet lined with parchment paper in a warm place until solid. Store in a screw-top jar or cardboard box lined with kitchen paper for several months.

Chocolate
&
Sugar

Chocolate varies greatly in quality, flavour and texture. There is now such a choice out there that it can be quite daunting to know which type to choose for baking, but this becomes clearer when you have an idea how chocolate is made and formed into bars of white, milk or plain chocolate.

Selecting chocolate

When the bitter cocoa beans have been roasted (similar to coffee beans, but at a lower temperature), they are cracked and the husks are removed – leaving behind the cocoa nibs. These nibs are ground into a thick paste and processed into cocoa butter and chocolate liquor (not the sweet variety). Different types of chocolate are then created, depending on the proportions used of cocoa butter and chocolate liquor.

White chocolate Made only from the cocoa butter and sugar with no addition of the chocolate liquor, hence the white colour and sweet flavour.

Plain chocolate Made from cocoa butter and chocolate liquor and sweetened with sugar. For baking and decorations look for a high percentage of cocoa solids (at least 70%). The plainer the chocolate, the harder the texture and the stronger the flavour will be.

Couverture chocolate At the top end of the chocolate quality scale and preferred by chefs for confectionery, couverture is made from cocoa butter and chocolate liquor with no added sugar. The end product is a very dark, brittle chocolate suitable only for chocolate work and cooking. This chocolate is ideal for hand-made chocolates, desserts, gâteaux and decorations. It must be tempered before use (see opposite).

Milk chocolate Made the same way as plain chocolate but with the addition of dried milk powder, which gives the chocolate a lighter colour and texture and a sweeter flavour.

Cocoa Made from the chocolate liquor that has been pressed and dried to form an unsweetened chocolate powder.

Other less expensive forms of chocolate are made with some of the cocoa butter replaced with vegetable fat. This makes the chocolate softer in texture and lacking in good flavour. There are guidelines in place for how much cocoa butter can be removed before the substance is no longer called chocolate.

Selecting chocolate

Melting chocolate

Care must be taken when melting chocolate since it is an exacting process and determines the set appearance of the chocolate, giving it either a smooth glossy finish or a dull streaked appearance. It is very important not to overheat any type of chocolate, as it will seize into an unusable mess. The bowl in which you are melting the chocolate must also be clean and dry.

Once melted, the chocolate may be used for dipping, coating, spreading, or for cut-out chocolate pieces (use tempered chocolate for this, see below) and piped decorations. Always choose a good-quality chocolate if melted chocolate is being used and set, as the flavour and texture is important.

To melt chocolate over a pan

Break or chop the chocolate and put it into a heatproof bowl. Set the bowl over a pan of barely simmering water (making sure the bowl does not touch the water, but sits above it and that there is no space between the bowl and the saucepan rim). The steam from the water will gently melt the chocolate – stir occasionally to evenly distribute the heat and do not try to hurry the process along or else the chocolate might seize and become unworkable.

To melt chocolate in a microwave

Put the broken or chopped chocolate into a microwave-safe bowl. Microwave on full power for 1 minute. Stir, then heat again in 10-second bursts until the chocolate is smooth and melted. If the temperature of the chocolate gets too high, it can seize or will dry with a streaked surface.

Melting chocolate over a pan

tip
If your chocolate has seized, try stirring in a few drops of flavourless vegetable oil.

Tempering chocolate

Tempering chocolate is a method of heating and cooling chocolate to particular temperatures that will ensure the chocolate dries with a hard, glossy finish.

For best results, chocolate should be tempered before using in moulds or to make decorations. If chocolate is melted without tempering, it will dry dull, grainy and quite soft. If adding chocolate to recipes, then it usually suffices to melt it as normal.

Always temper good-quality plain (or couverture), milk or white chocolates.

You will need an accurate and sensitive thermometer – a digital probe one is best.

1 Melt plain chocolate using one of the methods described above until it reaches 45°C. Milk and white chocolate should be heated to 43°C.
2 The chocolate must then be cooled to 27°C or 25°C for milk or white chocolate. To do this, simply place the bowl in a cool water bath (taking care that none of the water gets into the chocolate) and stir to keep the temperature even on cooling. Alternatively, add an additional 20% chopped chocolate to the melted bowl and stir to melt (this is called 'seeding').
3 Before using the chocolate, test that it is ready to use by dipping a metal palette knife into the chocolate and tapping off the excess. Leave to harden on the palette knife for 5 minutes – it should dry with a shiny appearance. If the chocolate is not shiny, repeat the tempering process.
4 Use to decorate or fill moulds. The temperature of the chocolate should remain between 27°C and 32°C (25°C and 30°C for milk and white chocolate) while you work.

Chocolate moulds

There are a huge number of wonderful chocolate moulds available, from teacups to rabbits and shoes to seashells. Sturdy paper or silicone cases also make good chocolate moulds. Ideally, use tempered chocolate for best results.

1 Pour melted tempered chocolate into a clean, dry mould. Turn the mould to coat it evenly with chocolate, then pour out the excess. Chill until set.
2 Repeat the process until you have the desired thickness (see notes). Leave to set, then turn the chocolate out, handling carefully.
3 Alternatively, use a small paintbrush to layer the chocolate. Simply dip the clean brush into the melted chocolate and paint the inside of the mould with it. Leave to set, then repeat layering with chocolate until you have achieved the desired thickness.

notes
• Your mould should not have awkward curves or angles, or you will not be able to release the chocolate from the mould.
• The larger the mould, the thicker the chocolate layer should be.

Pouring out excess chocolate from a mould

Chocolate moulds

Chocolate for dipping

This is ideal for small sweets, fruit and nuts. Strawberries are particularly good half-dipped in white chocolate.

1 Simply fully immerse or half-coat your chosen item in melted chocolate. If needed, use a toothpick or a small fork to lift the item out of the chocolate, then shake to remove any excess.
2 Leave to set on a baking tray lined with baking parchment. Trim off any excess cooled chocolate, to neaten, and use.

Chocolate for coating

This method can be used for cakes or biscuits. Ideally, use tempered chocolate for best results.

1 Stand cakes or biscuits on a wire rack, spaced apart. Put the rack over a large sheet of baking parchment (which will catch the drips).
2 Use a ladle to pour the chocolate over half, or the whole, cake or biscuit (or pour directly from the bowl, ensuring the base is completely dry).
3 Allow the excess chocolate to run on to the paper. Tap or gently shake the wire rack to level the chocolate. Scrape the chocolate from the baking parchment back into the bowl. Repeat the coating, if you wish, with another layer of chocolate after the first one has set.

Dipping fruit into melted chocolate

tip
White chocolate is very versatile and may be used for all chocolate work. It also lends itself to being coloured. Use only powdered food colourings, as any liquid added to the chocolate will cause it to thicken and become unusable.

Chocolate decorations

Chocolate decorations give an elegant, luxurious finish to cakes. Avoid over-handling the finished decorations, as they'll mark and melt easily. For best results on all decorations, use tempered chocolate (see page 91).

Chocolate wafers

1 You can make flat or curved wafers in any shape you like. Cut a piece of baking parchment to the desired width and length; alternatively, cut into individual shapes at this stage.
2 Brush the paper evenly with melted chocolate and leave until the chocolate has almost set. Using kitchen scissors or a knife, cut the chocolate sheet into pieces of the desired size and shape (if not already so).
3 Leave to cool and harden completely on a sheet of baking parchment, either flat or draped over something for curved results.
4 Using your fingers or a metal palette knife, carefully remove the wafers from the paper, handling them as little as possible, and store in the fridge for up to 24 hours.

Larger chocolate curls

1 Spread melted chocolate in a thin layer on a marble slab or clean work surface. Leave to firm up.
2 Using a sharp, flat-ended blade (such as a metal pastry scraper), push through the chocolate at a 45-degree angle. The size of the curls will be determined by the width of the blade.

Chocolate shavings

This is the easiest decoration of all because it doesn't call for melting chocolate. It's ideal for coating the sides and top of cakes. Use chilled chocolate.

1 Hold a chocolate bar upright on a work surface and shave pieces off the edge with a y-shaped vegetable peeler.
2 Alternatively, grate the chocolate against a coarse or medium-coarse grater to make very fine shavings.

Brushing melted chocolate onto paper

Peeling the chocolate from the paper

Using a scraper to make chocolate curls

Larger chocolate curls

Chocolate shavings made with a peeler

Chocolate shavings made with a grater

Spreading chocolate for the caraque

Painting leaves with melted chocolate

Brushing the paper with chocolate

Using a knife to form chocolate caraque

Peeling the leaf away from the chocolate

Cutting into triangles

Chocolate caraque (or fine curls)

The temperature of the set chocolate is important – keep testing the edge to see if it's ready.

1 Pour cooled, melted chocolate on to a marble slab or cool work surface. Using a palette knife, spread out the chocolate as evenly as possible to a thickness of 1–2mm (¹⁄₁₆ inch). Let the chocolate cool to almost setting point.

2 Using a metal pastry scraper or larger cook's knife held at a 45-degree angle against the marble or work surface, pull the blade towards you slowly to roll the chocolate into a cylinder. If the chocolate is too warm it will stick, if it is too cold it will only form shavings.

Chocolate leaves

1 Wash and dry some unsprayed rose or other non-toxic leaves, such as bay leaves. Using a small paintbrush, coat the shiny sides of the leaves with a layer of cooled, melted chocolate. Spread it right to the edges, but wipe off any chocolate that drips over the edge (as this can make peeling off the chocolate difficult).

2 Leave to set on a baking sheet lined with baking parchment in a cool, dry place.

3 When completely set, carefully peel away the leaves and store the chocolate leaves in the fridge in an airtight container between sheets of baking parchment for up to one month.

Chocolate triangles

1 Cut a length of silicone or baking parchment about 5cm (2 inches) wide. Brush with a layer of cooled, melted chocolate 1–2mm (¹⁄₁₆ inch) thick. Leave to cool to almost setting point.

2 Mark into triangles and leave to set but do not chill. For curved triangles, set the chocolate-coated paper along the length of a rolling pin or something similarly curved.

3 When the chocolate is completely set, carefully remove from the paper and store in the fridge in an airtight container between sheets of baking parchment for up to one month.

Piped chocolate decorations

Chocolate can be piped into decorative shapes to adorn cakes and cupcakes or piped directly on to cakes or cupcakes. Alternatively, use chocolate and hazelnut spread to pipe borders, as it is already an ideal consistency.

1 Draw your chosen design on to a piece of white paper or card. Tape a large piece of baking parchment over it – work on a flat surface where your decorations can be left to dry completely before moving.
2 Fill a greaseproof paper piping bag (see page 58) with chocolate that has been melted and allowed to cool and thicken slightly.
3 Holding the bag vertically, snip off the tip to the size of hole required and, using light pressure, pipe the chocolate on the outline or entirety of your design. Leave to set completely.
4 If you wish, fill in your design with a different colour of melted and cooled chocolate, then leave to set.
5 Using a metal palette knife, carefully remove the piped design. Store between sheets of baking parchment in an airtight container in the fridge for up to one month.

Modelling cocoform

Shop-bought modelling cocoform is made from chocolate and glucose, resulting in a pliable modelling material. It is ideal for making chocolate decorations, such as roses and frills. It can by moulded by hand or using templates. You

Piped chocolate decorations

can also mix cocoform with the same amount of sugarpaste or marzipan for a delicious flavoured cake covering. Cocoform is available in the more usual plain dark, milk and white chocolate varieties as well as in a selection of other colours and flavours (e.g. strawberry and cappuccino). Look for cocoform in specialist cake shops or via websites.

Chocolate – what went wrong

The chocolate has seized to during melting
- There was water in the bowl
- The melting chocolate has not been stirred to distribute the temperature
- Steam or water has dripped into the chocolate bowl
- The chocolate was overheated
- A cold liquid was added to the melted chocolate, which has 'shocked' it

The chocolate has a dull, streaky appearance
- The chocolate has passed its 'use-by' date
- The chocolate was stored at too high a heat
- It was not tempered properly before use
- The chocolate was chilled in the fridge and then left out at room temperature

The chocolate tastes bitter
- It was overheated and burned during heating

The chocolate has a grainy, unpleasant texture
- The chocolate has been exposed to excess humidity or moved from cold to hot temperatures quickly, which has caused the sugar to crystallise

There is a white bloom all over the chocolate
- The chocolate has passed its 'use-by' date and the cocoa butter has separated from the chocolate solids
- The chocolate has not been tempered properly

The chocolate is not melting well, despite gently heating
- The chocolate has been stored in the fridge or freezer and the condensation is causing the chocolate to seize

The chocolate smells rancid
- It has gone off

Working with sugar

Sugar is a wonderfully versatile ingredient. When heated it can be transformed entirely – into crisp caramel and praline and delicate spun sugar, to name but a few. When heating sugar, always do so in a heavy-based pan, wear long sleeves and use oven gloves.

Dry caramel

Use to make decorations. They can be made up to a few hours in advance and stored in an airtight container – but can turn sticky during this time depending on the atmosphere.

1 Line a baking sheet with lightly oiled greaseproof paper. Put 200g (7oz) caster sugar into a heavy-based pan with 4 tbsp water. Heat gently to dissolve.

2 Bring to the boil, then cook until it turns a medium caramel colour, swirling the pan to mix – it should be the colour of a dulled copper coin. Dip the base of the pan into cold water. Use the caramel immediately before the it begins to harden.

3 For caramel flowers, use a fork to drizzle flower shapes on to oiled greaseproof paper.

4 For caramel cages, lightly oil the back of a ladle. Drizzle caramel threads in a crisscross pattern over the ladle, finishing with a thread around the rim. Leave to set, and then carefully remove.

Liquid caramel

Caramel flowers

Caramel cages

Praline

Used as luminous shards or ground into rubble, praline is a cake decorator's dream.

250g (9oz) caster sugar

175g (6oz) nuts, such as walnuts or almonds

1 Put the sugar into a pan and warm over a gentle heat. Meanwhile, line a baking sheet with baking parchment.

2 Shake the pan gently to help dissolve the sugar, keeping a close eye on it when it starts to colour.

3 When the sugar has turned a dark golden brown, pour in the nuts and stir once with a wooden spoon. Working quickly, pour the praline on to the parchment and spread out. Leave to cool for 20 minutes.

4 Break the praline into shards by hitting with a rolling pin. Use as brittle shards, or whiz in a food processor to a fine powder. Perfect for dusting the sides of buttercream-iced cakes.

Praline

Spun sugar

One of the most attractive sugar decorations, spun sugar is made from a light caramel syrup spun into a nest of hair-thin threads. The only equipment you need is a pair of forks, a rolling pin and sheets of paper to catch any drips of syrup that fall on to the floor while you work.

1 Put the sugar and water into a pan, using 200g (7oz) caster sugar per 4 tbsp water. Heat gently until the sugar dissolves.

2 Turn the heat up to high and bring to the boil. Continue to boil until the sugar caramelises, swirling the pan to mix – you are looking for the colour of a dulled copper coin. Dip the bottom of the pan in cold water and leave to cool for 5 minutes.

3 Meanwhile, spread sheets of paper over the floor or table where you will be working.

4 Dip two or more forks, held in one hand, into the caramel. Flick them back and forth over a rolling pin held over the paper in your other hand, so that wispy threads fall over the pin.

5 When the rolling pin is full, carefully slide the threads off and gently form into a ball or keep them as threads. Use immediately to decorate cakes or desserts.

Spun sugar threads on a rolling pin

Spun sugar ball

Caramelising sugar – what went wrong

The water and sugar mixture has crystallised in the pan
- The sugar was not properly dissolved before boiling
- The pan was not clean
- There were impurities in the sugar
- The mixture was stirred when boiling

The sugar syrup is cloudy
- The mixture was boiled before the sugar dissolved
- The sugar and/or the pan wasn't clean

The sugar decorations have not set
- The sugar was not caramelised to a dark enough colour/high enough temperature
- The decorations have been left out at room temperature for too long and have started to melt

The sugar decorations are very sticky
- They have been left out at room temperature for too long and have started to melt.

The caramel is not forming thin threads when being spun
- The caramel is too hard
- The caramel is not being flicked fast enough

The sugar decorations taste bitter
- The caramel was taken too far and has burnt

The caramel is stuck fast to the pan
- Simply fill the pan with water and bring to the boil. The caramel will dissolve in the heat. Carefully tip out the water and wash as normal

Special Occasion Cakes

Chocolate Cake

Preparation: 30 minutes
Cooking time: 30 minutes, plus cooling

50ml (2fl oz) sunflower oil, plus extra to grease
75g (3oz) plain flour, plus extra to dust
250g (9oz) plain dark chocolate
(at least 70% cocoa solids), chopped
4 medium eggs
150g (5oz) light muscovado sugar
1 tsp vanilla extract
½ tsp baking powder

For the icing
100g (3½oz) plain dark chocolate
(at least 70% cocoa solids), chopped
300g (11oz) 2% fat Greek yogurt
1 tsp vanilla extract
100g (3½oz) icing sugar, sifted
raspberries

tip
This cake uses sunflower oil instead of butter, and far less of it.

1 Preheat the oven to 180°C (160°C fan oven) mark 4. Lightly grease two 20.5cm (8 inch) sandwich tins, then dust the insides with flour and tap out the excess.

2 Melt the chocolate in a heatproof bowl set over a pan of barely simmering water, making sure the base of the bowl is not touching the water. When melted and smooth, set aside to cool slightly.

3 Meanwhile, put the eggs into a large bowl and add the muscovado sugar, oil and vanilla extract. Using a hand-held electric whisk, beat the mixture until pale and thick – about 5 minutes. Sift the flour and baking powder into the egg bowl, then pour in the melted and cooled chocolate. Using a large metal spoon, fold together until combined.

4 Divide the mixture evenly between the prepared tins, level the surface and bake for 20 minutes, or until a skewer inserted into the centre of the cakes comes out clean. Leave the cakes to cool for 5 minutes, then remove from the tins and cool completely on a wire rack.

5 When the cakes are cool, make the icing. Melt the chocolate as before and set aside to cool for 10 minutes. In a medium bowl, mix the yogurt, vanilla and icing sugar, then stir in the melted and cooled chocolate. Keep mixing until the icing is thick and spreadable.

6 Put one of the cakes on a cake stand or plate, then spoon on some of the icing and spread to the edges. Top with the other cake. Spread the remaining icing over the top of the cake and cover with raspberries. Serve in slices.

Per slice
383 cals; 17g fat (of which 7g saturates);
56g carbohydrate; 0.2g salt

Afternoon Tea Carrot Cake

Preparation: 15 minutes

Cooking time: 40 minutes, plus cooling

250ml (9fl oz) sunflower oil,
plus extra to grease

225g (8oz) light muscovado sugar

3 large eggs

225g (8oz) self-raising flour

large pinch of salt

½ tsp each ground mixed spice, grated
nutmeg and ground cinnamon

250g (9oz) carrots, peeled and coarsely
grated

For the frosting

50g (2oz) butter, preferably unsalted,
at room temperature

225g pack cream cheese

25g (1oz) golden icing sugar

½ tsp vanilla extract

8 pecan halves, roughly chopped

1 Preheat the oven to 180°C (160°C fan oven) mark 4. Grease two 18cm (7 inch) sandwich tins and base-line with greaseproof paper, then grease the paper lightly.

2 Using a hand-held electric whisk, whisk the oil and muscovado sugar together to combine, then whisk in the eggs, one at a time.

3 Sift the flour, salt and spices together over the mixture, then gently fold in, using a large metal spoon. Tip the carrots into the bowl and fold in.

4 Divide the cake mixture between the prepared tins and bake for 30–40 minutes until golden and a skewer inserted into the centre comes out clean. Remove from the oven and leave in the tins for 10 minutes, then turn out on to a wire rack and leave to cool completely.

5 To make the frosting, beat the butter and cream cheese together in a bowl until light and fluffy. Sift in the icing sugar, add the vanilla extract and beat well until smooth. Spread one-third of the frosting over one cake and sandwich together with the other cake. Spread the remaining frosting on top and sprinkle with the pecans.

Per slice

383 cals; 32g fat (of which 10g saturates);
24g carbohydrate; 0.3g salt

Black Forest Birthday Gateau

cuts into 12 slices

Preparation: 30 minutes
Cooking time: 50 minutes,
plus cooling

125g (4oz) unsalted butter, melted
200g (7oz) plain flour
50g (2oz) cornflour
50g (2oz) cocoa powder, plus extra to dust
2 tsp espresso instant coffee powder
1 tsp baking powder
4 large eggs, separated
300g (11oz) golden caster sugar
2 × 300g jars morello cherries in syrup
2 tbsp Kirsch
200ml (7fl oz) double cream
2 tbsp icing sugar, sifted

For the decoration
fresh cherries
chocolate curls (see page 93)

note
Make the gateau up to two hours ahead to allow the flavours to mingle and the syrup to moisten the cake.

1 Preheat the oven to 180°C (160°C fan oven) mark 4. Brush a little of the melted butter over the base and sides of a 20.5cm (8 inch) round × 9cm (3½ inch) deep cake tin. Line the base and sides with baking parchment.

2 Sift the flour, cornflour, cocoa powder, coffee powder and baking powder together three times – this helps to add air and makes sure the ingredients are well mixed.

3 Put the egg yolks, caster sugar and 100ml (3½fl oz) cold water into a freestanding mixer and whisk for 8 minutes or until the mixture leaves a trail for 3 seconds when the whisk is lifted.

4 Add the rest of the melted butter, pouring it around the edge of the bowl so that the mixture doesn't lose any air, then quickly fold it in, followed by the sifted flour mixture in two batches.

5 In another bowl, whisk the egg whites until stiff peaks form, then fold a spoonful into the cake mixture to loosen. Carefully fold in the rest of the egg whites, making sure that there are no white blobs left. Pour into the prepared tin and bake in the oven for 45–50 minutes until a skewer inserted into the centre comes out clean. Leave in the tin for 10 minutes, then turn out on to a wire rack to cool completely.

6 When the cake is cold, trim the top to make a flat surface. Turn the cake over so that the top becomes the base. Using a long serrated bread knife, carefully cut horizontally into three. Drain the cherries, reserving 250ml (9fl oz) of the syrup. Put the syrup into a pan and simmer to reduce by half. Stir in the Kirsch. Brush the hot syrup on to each layer of the cake – including the top – using up all the liquid.

7 Lightly whip the cream with the icing sugar. Spread one-third over the bottom layer of cake and cover with half the cherries. Top with the next cake layer and repeat with another third of the cream and the remaining cherries. Top with the final cake layer and spread the remaining cream over. Decorate with fresh cherries, chocolate curls and a dusting of cocoa powder.

Per slice
440 cals; 22g fat (of which 12g saturates);
59g carbohydrate; 0.8g salt

Chocolate Birthday Cake

cuts into 12 slices

Preparation: 30 minutes, plus cooling
Cooking time: 1–1¼ hours, plus cooling

150ml (¼ pint) sunflower oil, plus extra
to grease

75g (3oz) creamed coconut

25g (1oz) plain chocolate, broken into pieces

50g (2oz) cocoa powder

350g (12oz) self-raising flour

1 tsp baking powder

pinch of salt

175g (6oz) light muscovado sugar

For the icing

350g (12oz) plain chocolate, broken into
small pieces

150ml (¼ pint) double cream

white and milk chocolate Maltesers to
decorate

1 Grease a 1.7 litre (3 pint), 30.5 × 10cm (12 × 4 inch) loaf tin and line with greaseproof paper. Put the coconut into a heatproof bowl, pour on 425ml (14½fl oz) boiling water and stir to dissolve. Set aside to cool for 30 minutes. Set aside to cool for 30 minutes.

2 Melt the chocolate in a heatproof bowl set over a pan of gently simmering water, making sure the base of the bowl doesn't touch the water. Stir until smooth, then remove the bowl from the pan and leave to cool slightly. Preheat the oven to 180°C (160°C fan oven) mark 4.

3 Sift the cocoa powder, flour, baking powder and salt into a bowl. Stir in the sugar and make a well in the middle. Add the coconut mixture, melted chocolate and oil and beat to make a smooth batter. Pour the cake batter into the prepared tin.

4 Bake for 1–1¼ hours or until risen and just firm to the touch (if necessary, after about 40 minutes, lightly cover the top of the cake with foil if it appears to be browning too quickly. Leave in the tin for 10 minutes, then transfer to a wire rack and leave to cool completely. When cold, trim to neaten the edges.

5 To make the icing, put the chocolate into a heatproof bowl. Heat the cream to just below boiling point. Pour on to the chocolate and stir until melted. Leave to cool, beating occasionally, until thick – pop into the fridge for 30 minutes to help thicken, if necessary.

6 Cut the cold cake in half horizontally and sandwich the layers together with one-third of the icing. Spread the rest evenly over the top and sides of the cake. Decorate the top of the cake with alternate rows of milk and white Maltesers. Lay an edging of alternate milk and white Maltesers around the base of the cake to decorate.

Per slice
515 cals; 31g fat (of which 15g saturates);
59g carbohydrate; 0.4g salt

Coffee and Praline Celebration Gateau

cuts into 8 slices

Preparation: 45 minutes
Cooking time: 25 minutes, plus cooling

50g (2oz) unsalted butter, melted, plus extra
to grease
125g (4oz) plain flour, sifted, plus extra to
dust
4 large eggs, separated
125g (4oz) caster sugar
1 tbsp coffee granules, dissolved in 2 tsp
boiling water

For the praline
50g (2oz) whole blanched hazelnuts
150g (5oz) caster sugar

For the filling
500g (1lb 2oz) mascarpone cheese
250g (9oz) icing sugar, sifted
2 tbsp coffee granules, dissolved in 1 tbsp
boiling water

1 Preheat the oven to 190°C (170°C fan oven) mark 5. Grease two 18cm (7 inch) loose-based sandwich tins. Dust lightly with flour and tip out the excess.
2 Put the egg whites into a clean, grease-free bowl and whisk until soft peaks form. Whisk in 1 egg yolk; repeat with the other 3 yolks. Add the sugar, 1 tbsp at a time, and continue to whisk. The mixture should be thick enough to leave a trail when the whisk is lifted. Using a large metal spoon, fold half the flour into the mixture.
3 Mix the coffee into the melted butter, then pour around the edge of the egg mixture. Add the remaining flour and gradually fold in. Divide the mixture between the prepared tins and bake for 25 minutes or until risen and firm to the touch. Turn out on to a wire rack and leave to cool completely.
4 To make the praline, line a baking sheet with non-stick baking parchment and scatter the nuts on it. Dissolve the sugar in a heavy-based pan over a low heat, shaking the pan once or twice to help it dissolve evenly. Cook until it forms a dark golden-brown caramel. Pour over the nuts and leave to cool.
5 To make the filling, put the mascarpone and icing sugar into a large bowl, add the coffee and mix with a hand-held electric whisk. Slice each cake in half horizontally. Put one cake layer on a plate and spread with a quarter of the filling. Continue layering in this way, finishing with a layer of mascarpone filling.
6 Break the praline into two or three pieces and put into a plastic bag. Using a rolling pin, smash it into smaller pieces. Use to decorate the top of the cake.

Per slice
548 cals; 21g fat (of which 10g saturates);
83g carbohydrate; 0.2g salt

White Chocolate Cappuccino Mother's Day Cake

cuts into 10 slices

Preparation: 45 minutes
Cooking time: about 50 minutes,
plus cooling

300g (11oz) unsalted butter, at room
temperature, plus extra to grease
250g (9oz) self-raising flour, plus extra
to dust
200g (7oz) caster sugar
3 large eggs, at room temperature, beaten
1½ tsp baking powder
50ml (2fl oz) milk
1 tsp vanilla extract
125g (4oz) white chocolate
125ml (4fl oz) double cream
1½–2 tbsp espresso coffee, cooled
75g (3oz) icing sugar, sifted, plus extra to
dust
50g (2oz) plain chocolate, grated
40g (1½oz) hazelnuts, roasted and chopped
fresh small roses to decorate

tip

For convenience, you can prepare ahead.
Make to the end of step 2 up to 24 hours
ahead. Return to the tin when cool and
wrap in clingfilm. Complete the recipe to
serve.

1 Preheat the oven to 180°C (160°C fan oven) mark 4. Grease a deep non-stick 20.5cm (8 inch) cake tin and dust with flour.
2 Beat together the caster sugar and 175g (6oz) butter until pale and creamy. Gradually add the eggs, beating well after each addition. Add 1 tbsp flour if the mix looks like curdling. Fold in the remaining flour and the baking powder, followed by the milk and vanilla extract. Spoon into the prepared tin and level the surface. Bake for 40–50 minutes until a skewer inserted into the centre comes out clean. Cool in the tin for 5 minutes, then turn out on to a wire rack and leave to cool completely.
3 Cut the cake in half horizontally. Grate 25g (1oz) white chocolate, then beat together with the cream and coffee until the mixture holds its shape. Use to sandwich the two cake halves together.
4 Melt the remaining white chocolate in a bowl set over a pan of simmering water, making sure the base doesn't touch the water. Leave to cool for 10 minutes. Beat together the remaining butter and the icing sugar until pale and creamy. Beat in the cooled white chocolate, then spread over the sides and top of the cake.
5 Mix the plain chocolate with the nuts and press around the side of the cake. Decorate with small roses dusted with icing sugar.

Per slice
659 cals; 45g fat (of which 25g saturates);
60g carbohydrate; 0.3g salt

Sachertorte

cuts into 12 slices

Preparation: 35 minutes
Cooking time: 45–55 minutes,
plus cooling and setting

175g (6oz) unsalted butter, at room
temperature, plus extra to grease
175g (6oz) golden caster sugar
5 medium eggs, lightly beaten
3 tbsp cocoa powder
125g (4oz) self-raising flour
225g (8oz) plain chocolate (at least 70%
cocoa solids), broken into pieces, melted
(see page 85) and cooled for 5 minutes
4 tbsp brandy
1 × quantity warm Rich Chocolate Ganache
(see tip)
12 lilac sugar-coated almonds, or 50g (2oz)
milk chocolate, melted, to decorate

tip
Rich chocolate ganache
Melt 175g (6oz) plain chocolate (at least
70% cocoa solids), broken into pieces,
with 75g (3oz) butter and 4 tbsp warmed
double cream in a heatproof bowl set
over a pan of gently simmering water,
making sure the base of the bowl doesn't
touch the water, stirring occasionally. Stir
the ganache until smooth.

1 Preheat the oven to 190°C (170°C fan oven) mark 5. Grease a 20.5cm (8 inch) springform cake tin and line with baking parchment.
2 Cream together the butter and sugar until pale and fluffy. Gradually beat in two-thirds of the beaten eggs – don't worry if the mixture curdles. Sift in the cocoa powder and 3 tbsp flour, then gradually beat in the remaining eggs. Fold in the remaining flour. Fold in the melted chocolate until evenly incorporated. Stir in 2 tbsp brandy. Pour the mixture into the prepared tin.
3 Bake for 45 minutes. If necessary, loosely cover the top of the cake with foil if it appears to be browning too quickly. To test if done, insert a skewer into the centre of the cake – it should come out clean. Cool in the tin for 30 minutes, then turn out on to a wire rack and leave to cool completely.
4 Drizzle with the remaining brandy, then position the wire rack over a tray. Ladle the ganache over the top of the cake, letting it trickle down the sides. Using a palette knife, spread it evenly over the cake. Decorate with almonds or melted milk chocolate and leave for about 1 hour to set.

Per slice
496 cals; 33g fat (of which 20g saturates);
45g carbohydrate; 0.7g salt

Simnel Cake

cuts into 12 slices

Preparation: 30 minutes, plus cooling
Cooking time: about 1 hour 25 minutes

225g (8oz) butter, softened, plus extra
to grease
225g (8oz) self-raising flour
2 tsp ground mixed spice
400g (14oz) mixed dried fruit
150g (5oz) light muscovado sugar
50g (2oz) golden syrup
finely grated zest of 2 lemons
4 medium eggs, lightly beaten

To decorate
icing sugar, to dust
500g (1lb 2oz) marzipan
2 tbsp apricot jam

You will also need
length of yellow ribbon

Per slice
546 cals; 23g fat (of which 11g saturates);
83g carbohydrate; 0.6g salt

1 Preheat the oven to 170°C (150°C fan) mark 3. Grease a 20.5cm (8 inch) round cake tin with butter and line with baking parchment.

2 In a large bowl, stir together the flour, mixed spice and dried fruit until combined. Put the butter, muscovado sugar, syrup and lemon zest into a separate large bowl and beat together using a hand-held electric whisk until pale and fluffy, about 3 minutes. Gradually beat in the eggs, whisking well after each addition. Add the flour mixture and fold everything together with a large metal spoon.

3 Empty the mixture into the prepared tin and bake, covering with foil after 1 hour of cooking, for 1 hour 25 minutes, or until the cake is risen and springy to the touch. A skewer inserted into the centre should come out clean, but don't be tempted to test too early or the cake may sink. Leave the cake to cool completely in the tin.

4 Take the cake out of the tin, peel off the parchment and transfer to a serving plate. To decorate, dust the work surface with icing sugar and roll out two-thirds of the marzipan until large enough for a 20.5cm (8 inch) circle (cut around the base of the cake tin). Heat the jam with 1 tsp water in a small pan over a medium heat until runny. Brush the top of the cake with some jam, then lay the marzipan circle on top and gently press down to stick it to the cake. Using a small knife, score lines on top of the cake to make a diamond pattern. Crimp the edge of the marzipan using the thumb and forefinger of one hand, and the index finger of the other.

5 Roll the remaining marzipan into 11 equal-sized balls. Brush the underside of each with a little jam or water and stick to the top of the cake. If you like, use a blowtorch to lightly brown the marzipan. To finish, secure a yellow ribbon around the side of the cake. Serve in slices.

note

Simnel cake is the classic Easter celebration cake, its marzipan balls representing the disciples – either 11 or 12 – depending on whether you think Judas should be included.

Easter Chocolate Fudge Cake

cuts into 12 slices

Preparation: 30 minutes
Cooking time: 50 minutes, plus cooling

175g (6oz) unsalted butter, softened,
plus extra to grease
150g (5oz) plain flour
50g (2oz) cocoa powder
1 tsp baking powder
pinch of salt
150g (5oz) light muscovado sugar
3 medium eggs, beaten
250ml (9fl oz) soured cream
1 tsp vanilla extract

For the icing and decoration
100g (3½oz) plain chocolate, finely chopped
150g (5oz) unsalted butter, softened
125g (4oz) cream cheese
175g (6oz) icing sugar, sifted
50g (2oz) chocolate curls, lightly crushed
(see page 93)
foil-covered chocolate eggs

1 Preheat the oven to 180°C (160°C fan oven) mark 4. Grease a 20.5cm (8 inch) springform tin and line with greaseproof paper, then grease the paper lightly. Sift the flour, cocoa powder, baking powder and salt into a large bowl.

2 Using an electric mixer or electric beaters, mix the butter and muscovado sugar in a separate bowl until pale and fluffy – about 5 minutes. Gradually add the beaten eggs, mixing well after each addition. Add a little of the flour mixture if the butter mixture looks like curdling. In one go, add the remaining flour mixture, the soured cream and vanilla extract, then fold everything together gently with a metal spoon. Spoon into the prepared tin and bake for 40–50 minutes until a skewer inserted into the centre comes out clean. Cool in the tin.

3 To make the icing, melt the chocolate in a heatproof bowl set over a pan of barely simmering water, making sure the base of the bowl doesn't touch the water. Leave to cool for 15 minutes. In a separate bowl, beat the butter and cream cheese with a wooden spoon until combined. Beat in the icing sugar, then the cooled chocolate. Take care not to over-beat the mixture – it should be fudgey, not stiff.

4 Remove the cake from the tin, cut in half horizontally and use some icing to sandwich the layers together. Transfer to a cake stand, then ice the top and sides, smoothing with a palette knife. Decorate with crushed curls and chocolate eggs.

Per slice
590 cals; 42g fat (of which 25g saturates);
50g carbohydrate; 0.7g salt

Red Velvet Cake

Preparation: 20 minutes

Cooking time: 1 hour 10 minutes,
plus cooling

200g (7oz) unsalted butter, softened,
plus extra to grease

250g (9oz) plain flour

40g (1½oz) cocoa powder

1½ tsp baking powder

225g (8oz) caster sugar

2 large eggs, beaten

250ml (9fl oz) soured cream

1 tbsp white wine vinegar

1 tsp bicarbonate of soda

¼ tsp red food colouring paste

For the frosting

400g (14oz) cream cheese

125g (4oz) unsalted butter, softened

125g (4oz) icing sugar

red sugar sprinkles to decorate (optional)

1 Preheat the oven to 180°C (160°C fan oven) mark 4. Grease a 20.5cm (8 inch) deep cake tin and line with parchment paper.

2 Sift the flour, cocoa powder and baking powder into a medium bowl. In a separate large bowl, beat together the butter and caster sugar with a hand-held electric whisk until pale and fluffy, about 5 minutes. Gradually beat in the eggs, until combined.

3 Alternately beat the flour mixture and the soured cream into the butter bowl until completely combined. Beat in the vinegar, bicarbonate of soda and food colouring. Spoon the mixture into the tin, level the surface and bake for 1 hour–1 hour 10 minutes until a skewer inserted into the centre comes out clean. Cool in the tin for 10 minutes, then turn out on to a wire rack and leave to cool completely.

4 To make the frosting, put the cream cheese and butter into a large bowl and beat together until combined. Sift in the icing sugar and mix well. Halve the cooled cake, then sandwich back together using half the icing. Spread the remaining icing over the top of the cake, decorate with sugar sprinkles, if you like, and serve in slices.

Per slice

724 cals, 53g fat (of which 33g saturates);
58g carbohydrate; 1.4g salt

Anniversary Cake

cuts into 10 slices

Preparation: 1½ hours
**Cooking time: 40 minutes, plus cooling,
setting and drying**

unsalted butter to grease
1 x Chocolate Victoria Sandwich mixture
(see page 30)
225g (8oz) chocolate ganache (see page 48)
1 tbsp Amaretto, rum or brandy
chocolate cigarillos (available from specialist
cake shops, websites or some supermarkets)
icing sugar to dust
petit four paper cases

note

What says 'happy anniversary' better than
a cake and box of chocolates in one? If
you don't have a heart-shaped tin, you can
make a square cake and carve out a heart.

tip

You will have more chocolate truffles than
will fit on top of the cake, but these will
keep well in the fridge for a couple of weeks
and make wonderful after-dinner treats.

1 Preheat the oven to 180°C (160°C fan oven) mark 4. Grease and line the base
and sides of a 1.1 litre (2 pint) heart-shaped tin. Spoon the chocolate cake
mixture into the prepared tin and bake until a skewer inserted into the centre
of the cake comes out clean, about 1 hour. Leave the cake to cool for 10
minutes in the tin, then transfer to a wire rack to cool completely.

2 Level the top of the heart cake a little, if needed, then slice the cake
horizontally into 3 even layers. Put one-third to a half of the chocolate
ganache into a bowl and stir in your chosen alcohol. Cover and chill.

3 Whip the remaining ganache until it is a spreadable consistency. Use some of
the ganache to sandwich the cake layers back together. Once reassembled,
spread a rough layer of ganache over the sides of the cake (this will support
the chocolate cigarillos) and a neat layer on top of the cake.

4 Trim the cigarillos to length (it looks nice if they are not all the same) and
stick to the sides of the cake. Shape some of the chilled ganache into round
truffles, dust in icing sugar and put into individual petit four cases
(alternatively, put the truffles straight on to the surface of the cake). Arrange
on the surface of the cake and serve.

Per slice
571 cals; 39g fat (of which 24g saturates);
53g carbohydrate; 0.5g salt

Toasted Hazelnut Meringue Birthday Cake

Gluten Free

cuts into 8 slices

Preparation: 10 minutes
Cooking time: 30 minutes,
plus cooling

oil to grease
175g (6oz) skinned hazelnuts, toasted
3 large egg whites
175g (6oz) golden caster sugar
250g carton mascarpone cheese
285ml (9½fl oz) double cream
3 tbsp Bailey's Irish Cream liqueur,
plus extra to serve
140g (4½oz) frozen raspberries
340g jar redcurrant jelly

1 Preheat the oven to 190°C (170°C fan oven) mark 5. Lightly oil two 18cm (7 inch) sandwich tins and base-line with baking parchment. Whiz the hazelnuts in a food processor until finely chopped.

2 Put the egg whites into a clean, grease-free bowl and whisk until stiff peaks form. Whisk in the sugar, a spoonful at a time. Using a metal spoon, fold in half the nuts. Divide the mixture between the tins and spread evenly. Bake in the middle of the oven for about 30 minutes, then leave to cool in the tins for 30 minutes.

3 To make the filling, put the mascarpone cheese into a bowl. Beat in the cream and liqueur until smooth. Put the raspberries and redcurrant jelly into a pan and heat gently until the jelly has melted. Sieve, then cool.

4 Use a palette knife to loosen the edges of the meringues, then turn out on to a wire rack. Peel off the baking parchment and discard. Put a large sheet of baking parchment on a board and sit one meringue on top, flat-side down. Spread one-third of the mascarpone mixture over the meringue, then drizzle with raspberry purée. Top with the other meringue, then cover the whole cake with the rest of the mascarpone mixture. Sprinkle with the remaining hazelnuts. Carefully put the cake on to a serving plate and drizzle with more liqueur, if you like.

Per slice
598 cals; 38g fat (of which 16g saturates);
57g carbohydrate; 0.1g salt

Baby Bunny Christening Cake

cuts into about 36 slices

To decorate: 1½ hours

about 500g (1lb 2oz) white sugarpaste
yellow and blue food colouring pastes
icing sugar, sifted, to dust
1 × 18cm (7 inch) square marzipanned and
sugarpasted rich fruit cake on a cake board
white royal icing (see page 43) made with
225g (8oz) icing sugar
alphabet letter sweets (optional)

tip
Remember to always keep any sugarpaste
not in use covered with clingfilm to stop
it drying out.

1 Colour 75g (3oz) white sugarpaste pale yellow and shape some of it into an oval body. Next, mould a slightly squashed round and, using a little water fix on to the body to make the bunny's head. Using a cocktail stick, press in holes to mark the eyes and pinch out a little icing to make the nose.

2 Using a little more of the yellow sugarpaste, mould and attach two arms to the body and two legs at the base, with flattened ovals for the feet. Use the remaining yellow sugarpaste to form the ears. Roll out a little white sugarpaste and cut out 2 small teardrop shapes to decorate the bunny ears. Fix to the ears with a little water, then fix the ears to the bunny head. Roll out a small amount of the white sugarpaste to make the mouth. Roll out a circle of white sugarpaste and stick onto the body. Add a small circle of white sugarpaste to each foot.

3 Colour half the remaining sugarpaste very pale blue. Lightly dust a work surface with icing sugar and roll out a small piece of the blue icing, then cut a small strip and make a bow to decorate the bunny's front. Fix in position with a little water.

4 Reroll the trimmings and roll out another small piece of blue icing to look like a blanket. Place on top of the cake and sit the bunny in the centre of the blanket. Leave to dry in position.

5 Roll out a little more of the blue sugarpaste and cut out an 18cm (7 inch) long, 2.5cm (1 inch) wide strip. Make sure the strip is lying flat, then roll a cocktail stick backwards and forwards across a short section of the edge until it frills. Repeat along the whole length of the strip. Attach the strip with a little water to one of the top edges of the cake, so that the frill sticks above the level of the icing. Repeat with the remaining three edges.

6 Colour the remaining white sugarpaste pale yellow. Roll out sections of yellow and blue icing to about 3mm (1/8 inch) thick. Cut out rough 2.5cm (1 inch) squares (they don't need to be very accurate). Press each square gently on to the surface of a grater, to give texture. Brush a section of the side of the cake (starting at the base) with water, and stick on squares in alternating colours. Carry on until all the sides are covered (you might need to colour some more icing depending on the depth of your cake/thickness of the squares).

7 To decorate the base of the cake, fit a piping bag with a star nozzle and fill with white royal icing. Hold the piping bag straight above the surface, with the nozzle just touching the surface. Press out some icing until you have the size of the star you want, meanwhile lifting the bag slightly to give the star space. Stop pressing, then pull up sharply to break the icing. Repeat next to the first star all around the cake to make a border.

8 Use alphabet letter sweets, if you like, to write the baby's name on top of the cake and stick them on with a little water. Leave to dry.

Per slice
395 cals; 11g fat (of which 4.5g saturates);
75g carbohydrate; 0.2g salt

Graduation Cake

cuts into about 20 slices

Preparation: 1½ hours
Cooking time: about 40 minutes,
plus cooling, setting and drying

unsalted butter to grease
2 × base carrot cake mixture (see page 101)
about 150g (5oz) white sugarpaste,
plus extra to cover the board
1½ × 50g (2oz) butter quantity carrot cake
frosting (see page 101)
icing sugar, sifted, to dust
500g (1lb 2oz) plain chocolate cocoform
(see page 95)
thick glacé icing to pipe

You will also need
large square cake board
sheet of rice paper
ribbon (optional)

tip
Cocoform (or modelling chocolate) is
available from specialist cake shops or
via websites.

1 Preheat the oven to 180°C (160°C fan oven) mark 4. Grease and line two 20.5cm (8 inch) square roasting tins (they don't need to be very deep). Make up the carrot cake mixture and divide between the prepared tins. Bake for 40 minutes or until a skewer inserted into the centre comes out clean. Leave to cool in the tins for 10 minutes, then transfer to a wire rack to cool completely.

2 Meanwhile, cover the cake board in white sugarpaste (see page 54) and leave to harden.

3 Trim each cake into a book-shaped rectangle and cut both rectangles in half horizontally. Use some of the frosting to sandwich the rectangles back together, then lightly cover each with more frosting. Leave to set for 30 minutes.

4 Lightly dust a work surface with icing sugar and roll out half of the white sugarpaste to about a 5mm (¼ inch) thickness. Cut into a strip slightly wider than the depth of the cake, and long enough to wrap around two of the short sides and one long side of the cake. Use a knife to mark the strip into what looks like pages. Wrap the strip around the cake (one long side should be left free). Repeat the process with the other cake.

5 Roll out about 250g (9oz) cocoform until it is about 5mm (¼ inch) thick. Cut out a wide strip long enough to cover the top, one side and back of one cake. Position the strip on to the cake, press down lightly and trim any excess. Roll out the remaining cocoform and repeat to cover the other cake. Leave to dry.

6 When the cakes have hardened, stack on the iced cake board. Use a little thick glacé icing to pipe subjects on the spines of the books, and a message on the board, if you like. Roll up some rice paper and tie with the ribbon to make a scroll. Fix on to the books with a little glacé icing. Leave the cake to dry.

Per slice
613 cals; 38g fat (of which 13g saturates);
67g carbohydrate; 0.6g salt

Fresh Flower Wedding Cake

To decorate: 45 minutes
1 × 15cm (6 inch), 1 × 20.5cm (8 inch) and
1 × 25.5cm (10 inch) round marzipanned and
sugarpasted rich fruit cakes
extra sugarpaste (optional)

You will also need:
dowels
1 × 15cm (6 inch), 1 × 20.5cm (8 inch) and
1 × 25.5cm (10 inch) round cake boards
polystyrene dummies – 12.5cm (5 inch) and
7.5cm (3 inch) were used in this cake
ribbon (optional)
fresh flowers
florists' wire (optional)
toothpick or skewer (optional)
flower pick (optional)

tip
When using fresh flowers on a wedding
cake, since they will be in close contact
with the cake, always buy non-toxic
flowers that have not been treated with
chemicals. Roses, gerbera and hydrangeas
work particularly well and give a good
visual result.

1 Measure and dowel your base-layer sugarpasted cake (which should be
on a cake board) to the same dimensions as the polystyrene dummy. The
dummy needs to be a good few inches smaller than the cake on which it is
sitting but the size varies depending on the depth of the flower, the size of
the cake and the desired end result. As a general guide the dummy should
be 7.5cm (3 inch) smaller than the tier it is supporting.
2 Sit the dummy centrally on the base layer of cake and top with the next layer
of the sugarpasted cake (which also needs to be on a cake board). Repeat the
process, if necessary, with another dummy and a final top tier. Cover the
edges of the cake boards with ribbon if they are showing. Trim the cakes
with other ribbons, as you like. Disassemble the cake and store until needed.
3 On the day of the celebration prepare your fresh flowers. Trim the stems of
the flowers (if necessary) to about 5cm (2 inch) and split any larger blooms
(such as hydrangeas) into smaller, more regular sections. Wrap the stems
with florists' wire to strengthen them if necessary – roses and other hardier
flowers are stiff enough, whereas gerberas will need strengthening.
4 Stack the cakes with the dummies in between the layers. Now insert the
flowers into the dummies (you might need to poke a hole into the dummy
with a toothpick or skewer to help the flower insertion), filling until you
can no longer see any polystyrene.
5 If you want to top your cake with more fresh flowers, either use a flower pick
or press a lump of soft sugarpaste on to the top tier, then insert flowers into
the sugarpaste. To prevent the flowers from wilting, make sure the cake is
kept out of direct sunlight.

Using polystyrene dummies
If you wish to display a lot of fresh flowers on a wedding cake without using numerous
flower picks (see below), then polystyrene dummies are the answer. These can be
stuffed with fresh flowers, which will give the effect of floating floral layers between
sugarpasted cakes.

Using flower picks
Avoid sticking the stems of the flowers straight into the sugarpasted cake, as you run the
risk of introducing germs. Instead, use food-safe flower picks that can be inserted into your
cake and safely hold flowers in position (see left). Flower picks are available in a range of
sizes and shapes from specialist cake shops or websites and can hold anything from a single
stem to a larger spray.

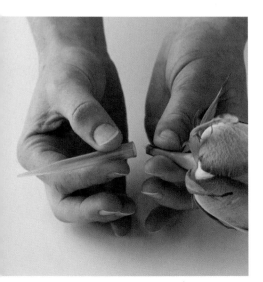

*Attaching a flower pick to the stem of
a rose*

White Chocolate and Orange Wedding Cake

cuts into 30 slices

Preparation: 1½ hours, plus chilling
Cooking time: 1 hour, plus cooling

butter to grease
550g (1¼lb) strawberries, hulled and thinly sliced

For the large cake
6 large eggs, separated
250g (9oz) golden caster sugar
150g (5oz) self-raising flour
150g (5oz) ground almonds
grated zest of 2 oranges

For the medium and small cakes
4 large eggs, separated
165g (5½oz) golden caster sugar
125g (4oz) self-raising flour
125g (4oz) ground almonds
grated zest of 1¼ oranges

For the syrup
200g (7oz) golden granulated sugar
500ml (18fl oz) sweet white wine
juice of 6 large oranges

For the white chocolate ganache
400g (14oz) white chocolate, chopped
600ml, 300ml and 150ml cartons double cream

1 Preheat the oven to 180°C (160°C fan oven) mark 4. Grease and base-line with greaseproof paper a deep, round 23cm (9in) cake tin, a 15cm (6in) cake tin and a 200g clean baked-bean tin.

2 To make the large cake, put the egg whites into a clean, grease-free bowl and whisk until soft peaks form. Gradually beat in 50g (2oz) sugar. Whisk until the mixture stands in stiff peaks and looks glossy.

3 Put the egg yolks and remaining sugar in another bowl and whisk until soft and moussey. Carefully stir in the flour to make a paste.

4 Using a clean metal spoon, add a third of the egg white to the paste and fold in carefully. Put the remaining egg white, the ground almonds and orange zest into the bowl and fold in, taking care not to knock too much volume out of the egg white. You should end up with a smooth batter.

5 Spoon into the prepared 23cm (9in) tin and bake for 35 minutes or until a skewer inserted into the centre comes out clean.

6 Cool in the tin for 10 minutes, then turn out on to a wire rack and leave to cool completely. Make the other two cakes in the same way, gradually beating in 25g (1oz) of the sugar at step 2. Pour a quarter of the batter into the baked bean tin and the remaining mixture into the 15cm (6in) cake tin. Bake the medium cake for 30–35 minutes and the small cake for 25–30 minutes. Turn out and cool as before.

7 Put the syrup ingredients into a pan and stir over a gentle heat until the sugar has dissolved. Bring to the boil and bubble for 5 minutes or until syrupy. Cool and set aside.

8 To make the ganache, put the chocolate into a heatproof bowl with half the cream. Set over a pan of simmering water, making sure that the base of the bowl doesn't touch the water, and leave until the chocolate has melted, then stir. Don't stir the chocolate until it has completely melted. Leave to cool until beginning to thicken, then beat with a wooden spoon until cold and thick. Put the remaining double cream into a bowl and whip lightly. Beat a large spoonful of the whipped cream into the chocolate cream to loosen it, then fold in the remainder. Cover and leave to chill for 2 hours.

9 Cut the cakes in half horizontally, pierce all over with a skewer and put them, cut-sides up, on an edged tray or baking sheet. Spoon the syrup over and leave to soak in.

10 Spread a quarter of the ganache over the base cakes and scatter with 425g (15oz) strawberries. Cover with the top half of each cake and press down lightly. Using a palette knife, smooth the remaining ganache over the top and sides of the cakes. Assemble up to 4 hours ahead, wrap loosely and keep chilled in the fridge. Decorate with the remaining strawberries and serve.

variation

Single-tiered celebration cake Make the larger cake only, then split it and drizzle with syrup made with 100g (3½oz) golden granulated sugar, 250ml (8fl oz) sweet white wine and the juice of 3 large oranges. Use 350g (12oz) strawberries for the filling and decoration. Fill, then cover, with ganache made from 225g (8oz) white chocolate and a 568ml carton double cream.

Per slice

530 cals; 34g fat (of which 17g saturates);
49g carbohydrate; 0.3g salt

Rosebud Wedding Cake

cuts into 180–200 small slices

Preparation: at least 1 day, plus drying

250g (9oz) sugar flower paste (available from cake decorating suppliers)

pink food colouring

5kg (11lb) white sugarpaste

white royal icing (see page 43) made with 225g (8oz) icing sugar

1 × 30.5cm (12 inch) round Traditional Rich Fruit Cake (see pages 28–9), covered in almond paste set on a 40.5cm (16 inch) cake board (drum)

1 × 23cm (9 inch) round Traditional Rich Fruit cake, covered in almond paste set on a 23cm (9 inch) cake board (double thick)

1 × 15cm (6 inch) round Traditional Rich Fruit cake, covered in almond paste set on a 15cm (6 inch) cake board (double thick)

You will also need

no. 2 and no. 3 piping nozzles

6 plastic cake dowels

pink ribbon

fresh pink roses (optional)

1 To make sugar roses, colour the flower paste different shades of pale pink. Make a cone shape a bit smaller than the size of the petal. Roll the flower paste out thinly, using only small amounts at a time, and cut out a 5-petal rose shape with a cutter. Thin the edges of the petals slightly with a bone tool, or roll them over a cocktail stick.

2 Dampen the lower part of each petal with a little water and wrap the petals around the cone one at a time, slightly overlapping each petal as you go. Repeat with a second set of 5 petals. Using your fingers, curl the outer edges of the petals to give a natural rose shape. Repeat to make at least 12 roses. Use a smaller cutter to make at least 24 roses for the sides of the cakes. Leave overnight to harden.

3 Take the largest cake on its cake board. Roll out some of the sugarpaste so that it is 4–5mm (¼ inch) thick and large enough to cover the cake. Dampen the cake with a little boiled water. Lift the icing on to the cake and smooth over the top and sides, trimming the excess icing away around the base. Dampen the surrounding cake board. Roll out a long thin strip of icing to cover the board and trim away the excess. Ice the two smaller tiers in the same way.

4 Cut a circle of greaseproof paper to the size of the top of each cake. Fold the largest two into 8 segments, the smallest into 6 segments. Using a compass or the bottom of a glass with the right diameter, pencil a scallop on the rounded edge between the folds about 5cm (2 inches) deep for the larger cakes and 2.5cm (1 inch) deep for the top tier. Cut out the scallops.

5 Open out the paper and place the smallest piece in the centre of the smallest cake and the two larger pieces in the centre of the two larger cakes. Hold the paper with one hand while pricking the scalloped outline on to the icing.

6 For the side scallops, cut a strip of greaseproof paper the circumference of the cake. As before, fold into 8 segments and mark the scallops in the same way. Remove the paper and, using an icing bag fitted with the plain no. 3 icing nozzle and filled with white royal icing, pipe a line of icing along the line of the scallops. Leave to dry for about 1 hour before piping a second, thinner line on top of the first using the no. 2 nozzle.

7 Push three dowels into each of the two larger cakes (see page 71). Using a pencil, mark the dowels where they are level with the top of the cake. Remove the dowels and cut each one where marked. However, if the top of the cake is not completely flat, make sure the three dowels are cut to equal length otherwise the cake above may slope. Push the dowels back into the holes. Carefully stack the middle and top cakes.

8 Secure a piece of ribbon around each cake with a small dot of royal icing.

9 Complete the decoration by piling up the large icing roses on the centre of the top cake and placing a smaller rose at each of the points where the scallops meet. Surround with fresh roses and petals, if you like.

Per slice
555 cals; 16g fat (of which 5g saturates); 92g carbohydrate; 0.2g salt

Classic Christmas Cake

cuts into 24 slices

Preparation: 30 minutes, plus soaking
Cooking time: about 4 hours, plus cooling

500g (1lb 2oz) sultanas
400g (14oz) raisins
150g (5oz) each Agen prunes and dried figs,
roughly chopped
200g (7oz) dried apricots, roughly chopped
zest and juice of 2 oranges
200ml (7fl oz) hazelnut liqueur, such as
Frangelico Hazelnut Liqueur, plus extra
to drizzle
250g (9oz) unsalted butter, softened,
plus extra to grease
150g (5oz) each dark muscovado and light
brown soft sugar
200g (7oz) plain flour, sifted
1 tsp ground cinnamon
1 tsp mixed spice
¼ tsp ground cloves
¼ tsp freshly grated nutmeg
pinch of salt
4 large eggs, beaten
100g (3½oz) toasted, blanched hazelnuts,
roughly chopped
40g (1½oz) toasted pinenuts
1 tbsp brandy (optional)

Per slice (un-iced)
373 cals; 14g fat (of which 6g saturates);
50g carbohydrate; 0.4g salt

icing: makes enough to cover a 23cm (9 inch) cake

Preparation: 30 minutes, plus drying
Cooking time: 3–4 minutes, plus cooling

4 tbsp apricot jam
1 fruit cake (see above)
icing sugar, sifted, to dust
450g packet ready-to-roll marzipan
vegetable oil to grease
150g (5oz) glacier mint sweets
500g packet royal icing sugar

You will also need
75 × 2cm (30 × ¾ inch) silver ribbon
silver candles

Per serving (including cake)
569 cals; 17g fat (of which 6g saturates);
100g carbohydrate; 0.2g salt

1 Put the fruit into a non-metallic bowl and stir in the orange zest and juice and the hazelnut liqueur. Cover and leave to soak overnight or, preferably, up to three days.

2 Preheat the oven to 140°C (120°C fan oven) mark 1. Grease a 23cm (9 inch) cake tin and double-line with greaseproof paper, making sure the paper comes at least 5cm (2 inches) above the top of the tin. Grease the paper lightly. Then wrap a double layer of greaseproof paper around the outside of the tin, securing with string – this will stop the cake burning.

3 Using a hand-held electric mixer, beat together the butter and sugars in a large bowl until light and fluffy – this should take about 5 minutes.

4 In a separate bowl, sift together the flour, spices and salt. Beat 2 tbsp of the flour mixture into the butter and sugar, then gradually add the eggs, making sure the mixture doesn't curdle. If it looks as if it might be about to, add a little more flour.

5 Using a large metal spoon, fold the remaining flour into the mixture, followed by the soaked fruit and the nuts. Tip into the prepared tin and level the surface. Using the end of the spoon, make a hole in the centre of the mix, going right down to the base of the tin – this will stop the top of the cake rising into a dome shape as it cooks. Bake for 4 hours or until a skewer inserted into the centre comes out clean. Cover with foil if it is browning too quickly. Leave to cool in the tin for 10 minutes, then turn out on to a wire rack, keeping the greaseproof paper wrapped around the outside of the cake, and leave to cool completely.

6 To store, leave the cold cake in its greaseproof paper. Wrap a few layers of clingfilm around it, then cover with foil. Store in a cool place in an airtight container. After two weeks, unwrap the cake, prick all over and pour over 1 tbsp of hazelnut liqueur, or brandy if you prefer. Rewrap and store as before. Ice up to three days before serving (see below).

Icing the cake

1 Gently heat the jam in a pan with 1 tbsp water until softened, then press through a sieve into a bowl to make a smooth glaze. Put the cake on a board and brush over the top and sides with the glaze.

2 Dust a rolling pin and the work surface with a little icing sugar and roll out the marzipan to a round about 15cm (6 inches) larger than the cake. Position over the cake and ease to fit around the sides, pressing out any creases. Trim off the excess around the base. Leave to dry for 24 hours.

3 Preheat the oven to 180°C (160°C fan oven) mark 4. Line a baking sheet with foil and brush lightly with oil. Unwrap the mints and put pairs of sweets on the baking sheet about 1cm (½ inch) apart, leaving 5cm (2 inches) of space between each pair, to allow room for them to spread as they melt. Cook for 3–4 minutes until the sweets have melted and are just starting to bubble around the edges. Leave to cool on the foil for 3–4 minutes until firm enough to be lifted off. Use kitchen scissors to snip the pieces into large slivers and shards.

4 Wrap the ribbon around the edge of the cake. Put the icing sugar in a bowl and make up according to the pack instructions. Using a small palette knife, spread the icing over the top of the cake, flicking it into small peaks as you go. Then tease the edges of the icing down the sides of the cake to form icicles.

5 While the icing is still soft, push the mint shards into the top of the cake and insert the silver candles. Leave the cake to dry. Light the candles and serve.

Novelty Cakes

Sleeping Beauty's Castle

cuts into 35 small slices

Preparation: 1 hour

1 × white ready-iced square 23cm (9 inch)
sponge cake

5 raspberry or strawberry Swiss rolls, about
9cm (3½ inch) long

450g (1lb) white sugarpaste

icing sugar to dust

apricot glaze (see page 49)

1 × white ready-iced round 15cm (6 inch)
sponge cake

2 × quantities of pink buttercream icing
(see page 48)

5 ice cream sugar cones

For the decoration

multicoloured sprinkles

red, pink, yellow, green and white
writing icing

sugar flowers

small round pink sweets or pink edible balls

paper flag

You will also need

1 × 30.5cm (12in) square cake board

note

For convenience, complete the recipe up
to one day in advance.

1 Put the square cake on the 30.5cm (12 inch) square cake board. Measure the circumference of a Swiss roll with a piece of string. Divide the sugarpaste into five pieces. Lightly dust a work surface with icing sugar, then roll out each piece of sugarpaste thinly into a rectangle the length of the Swiss roll by the length of the piece of string. Neaten the edges with a sharp knife. Brush each piece of icing with apricot glaze and roll around a Swiss roll, gently working the edges together to seal.

2 Put the round cake in the centre of the square cake. Put a dollop of buttercream at each corner of the square cake and position four of the Swiss rolls, with the sealed edge facing inwards, to make towers. Smooth pink buttercream over four of the cones and spread a little on top of each tower. Dip the tips of the cones in sprinkles, then fix on top of the towers. Using red writing icing, draw a simple window, divided by four panes, at the top of each tower.

3 At the front of the castle, use red writing icing to draw a door with a doorknob. Use pink and yellow writing icing to draw small flowers around the castle and below the windows. Fix a few sugar flowers to the walls with writing icing. Connect the flowers with green writing icing to represent stems. Use the green writing icing to draw clumps of grass around the base of the wall. Stick a sugar flower to the paper flag with writing icing.

4 Position the remaining Swiss roll in the centre of the round cake. Cover the remaining cone with buttercream, dip in sprinkles and position on top of the round cake, fixing with a little buttercream. Draw on windows and decorate with sugar flowers as before. Make blobs of white writing icing, just touching each other, around the edges of the cones and decorate with pink sweets or edible balls. Stick the paper flag into the central tower.

Per slice

425 cals; 8g fat (of which 3g saturates);
86g carbohydrate; 0.2g salt

Creepy-crawly Cake

cuts into 12 slices

Preparation: 1½ hours
Cooking time: 25–30 minutes,
plus cooling and drying

butter to grease
1 × 4-egg quantity of chocolate Victoria
sponge mixture (see page 30)
½ × quantity of chocolate buttercream icing
(see page 48)

For the decoration
225g (8oz) white sugarpaste
assorted food colourings, including brown
and black
red and black liquorice bootlaces and jelly
creepy-crawly sweets, such as snakes and
frogs
a little glacé icing (see page 43)
a chocolate matchstick (optional)

For the icing
450g (1lb) icing sugar, sifted
225g (8oz) butter, softened
a few drops of vanilla extract
green food colouring

1 To make a trap door, use 125g (4oz) sugarpaste. Knead in a few drops of brown food colouring and roll out to a thickness of 5mm (¼ inch), then use a small tumbler to cut out a circle. Place on a baking tray lined with baking parchment and leave in a cool place overnight to dry.

2 Use the remaining white and brown icing to make a selection of spiders and beetles, colouring the icing accordingly. Use the liquorice to make spiders' legs. Pipe eyes on the creatures with white glacé icing. Allow to dry overnight.

3 The next day, preheat the oven to 190°C (170°C fan oven) mark 5. Grease two 20.5cm (8 inch) round sandwich tins and line with greaseproof paper, then grease the paper lightly. Make and bake the sponge mixture according to the instructions on page 28. Cool in the tins for 5 minutes, then turn out on to a wire rack, remove the lining paper and leave to cool completely.

4 Sandwich the cold cakes together with chocolate buttercream. Cut out a hole 1cm (½ inch) deep and 6.5cm (2½ inches) wide in the centre of the cake. Discard (or eat) the trimmings.

5 For the icing, beat the icing sugar into the butter with the vanilla. Beat in the food colouring. Put the cake on a board or plate and cover with the icing. Secure the trap door over the hole in the middle of the cake. Prop open with a cocktail stick painted with brown food colouring, or a chocolate matchstick. Arrange the creatures over the cake, with some creepy-crawlies crawling out of the trap door. Leave to dry.

Per slice
534 cals; 26 fat (of which 17g saturates);
76g carbohydrate; 0.6g salt

Clown Cake

cuts into 15 slices

Preparation: 45 minutes

25g (1oz) each of white, green, black and blue
sugarpaste
50g (2oz) red sugarpaste
black and yellow writing icing
1 × white ready-iced 20.5cm (8 inch) sponge
cake

1 First make the shapes for the clown's face. Roll out the white sugarpaste
   and cut out two ovals for eyes. Roll out half the red sugarpaste and cut out
   a crescent shape for the mouth. Mark a smiley line along the centre of the
   mouth with black writing icing. Knead the trimmings and the other piece
   of red icing together and roll into a ball for his nose. Roll out a small piece
   of green icing and, using a star-shaped cutter, stamp out two stars for
   his cheeks.
2 Brush the backs of the shapes with water and position on the cake. Roll out
   the black icing and cut out two small circles to make pupils for the eyes, then
   stick on to the white ovals. Use the black and yellow writing icing to give him
   eyebrows and a swirl of hair.
3 Roll out the blue icing and cut out two sides of a bow tie. Roll the trimmings
   into a ball and flatten slightly to make the centre knot. Fix the two bow-tie
   pieces to the bottom edge of the cake with writing icing. Position the knot on
   top. Use the yellow writing icing to pipe polka dots on the tie.

Per slice
300 cals; 8g fat (of which 2g saturates);
55g carbohydrate; 0.1g salt

cuts into about 16 slices
(or more for little mouths!)

Preparation: 1½ hours
Cooking time: about 1½ hours,
plus cooling, setting and drying

unsalted butter to grease
1 x 18cm (7 inch) round cake tin quantity
Madeira cake mixture (see page 34)
100–125g (3½–4oz) white sugarpaste
pink food colouring paste
lustre dust (optional)
edible glue (optional)
500g (1lb 2oz) buttercream (see page 48)
400g (14oz) vanilla frosting (see page 46)
pink sugar crystals (optional)

You will also need
4 short lengths of pale pink satin ribbon
1 cake stand

tip
Inspired by the many layers of a ballerina
tutu, this cake is sure to delight any
young girl. You will need a petal nozzle
(shaped like a narrow teardrop) to create
these dramatic ruffles.

1 Preheat the oven to 170°C (150°C fan oven) mark 3. Grease and line a deep 18cm (7 inch) round cake tin. Make the Madeira cake mixture, fill the tin and bake for 1¼–1½ hours until the cake is golden on top and a skewer inserted into the centre comes out clean. Leave to cool for 10 minutes in the tin, then take out and cool completely on a wire rack.

2 While the cake is cooling, tint the sugarpaste to a very light pink (ballet slipper colour). Divide the sugarpaste in half and roll one of the halves into a sausage shape. Using your fingers, press into the top of the sausage shape to form a slipper, making sure you leave the cap of the shoe in place. Make the slipper narrower in the middle and as delicate as possible. Brush the slipper with lustre dust and, with the help of a small knife, insert two short lengths of ribbon in place (alternatively stick the ribbon to the outside of the shoes with edible glue). Put on to a sheet of baking parchment. Repeat with the other slipper and leave them to dry for at least 3 hours (or make the day before and allow to dry overnight).

3 Slice the cooled cake into three even layers. Dye the buttercream to a darker shade of pink. Sandwich the cake layers back together using some of the buttercream. Put the cake on a turntable. Lightly spread buttercream on the sides, then cover the top generously and neatly. Leave to set for 30 minutes, then transfer to a cake stand.

4 Dye 350g (12oz) vanilla frosting pale pink. Fit a piping bag with a petal leaf nozzle and fill with the frosting. Holding the bag nearly vertical so that the tip (narrow end facing outwards) is by the base of the cake, create a ruffle by squeezing the bag while making a 2.5cm (1 inch) wide quick back and forth motion, at the same time moving the nozzle up the side of the cake. Finish the ruffle at the top edge of the cake, pulling off as neatly as possible. Repeat ruffling all around the cake.

5 Sprinkle pink sugar crystals, if using, over the top of the cake. Dye the remaining white frosting to just a hint of pink and pipe a border around the top edge of the cake, then position the slippers and ribbons. Leave to dry.

Per slice
463 cals; 20g fat (of which 11g saturates);
73g carbohydrate; 0.4g salt

cuts into 12 slices

Preparation: 1½ hours
Cooking time: 40 minutes, plus cooling

unsalted butter to grease
1 × 3-egg quantity of Victoria sponge mixture
(see page 30)
700g (1½lb) white sugarpaste
brown, red, green and yellow food colourings
½ × quantity of buttercream icing
(see page 48)
cornflour to dust
sugar flowers, dolly mixtures and butterfly
decorations

You will also need
1 large rectangular cake board

1 Preheat the oven to 190°C (170°C fan oven) mark 5. Grease a 900g (2lb) food can and a 1.1 litre (2 pint) pudding basin and base-line with baking parchment. It doesn't matter how big the basin is, as long as it holds at least 1.1 litres (2 pints). A wide, shallow cake makes a better-looking toadstool.

2 Make the cake mixture according to the instructions on page 28. Half-fill the food can and put the remaining mixture into the pudding basin. Bake for about 30 minutes for the 'stalk' in the food can and 40 minutes for the 'mushroom cap' in the pudding basin. Transfer both to a wire rack and leave to cool.

3 Take 350g (12oz) sugarpaste. Colour a walnut-sized piece with brown food colouring and the rest red. Colour 125g (4oz) green and leave the remaining 225g (8oz) white. Roll out the green icing and cut into a kidney shape as a 'grass' base. Fix to a cake board with a little water. Unmould the cakes. Using the food can that the stalk was baked in as a template, cut a semi-circle from one side of the grass.

4 Reserve 50g (2oz) white icing. Colour the rest yellow and roll out into a long oblong to fit the stalk. Trim the edges. Spread buttercream thinly around the stalk cake then, holding the cake by the ends, set it at one end of the icing. Roll up the icing around the stalk and press the seam together. With a dab of buttercream, fix the stalk upright in the cut-out semi-circle in the green icing. Spread the top with buttercream.

5 Roll out the red icing to fit the mushroom cap. Set the cake flat on the work surface. Cover the upper surface thinly with buttercream. Lay the red icing over the cake. Smooth in place and trim around the base. Dust the work surface lightly with cornflour and carefully turn the cake upside down.

6 Colour the remaining buttercream dark brown. Insert a small, fluted nozzle into a piping bag. Fill the bag with the buttercream. Mark a circle in the centre of the base of the mushroom cap, where the stalk will fit. Pipe lines of buttercream radiating from this, to look like the 'gills' of a toadstool. Cover the sponge and red icing join. Turn the cake the right way up and set on top of the stalk. Roll out the reserved white icing and the brown icing. Cut the white icing into dots. Arrange on top of the toadstool, using a little buttercream to fix them. Cut the brown icing into windows and a door and fix to the stalk in the same way. Decorate the 'grass' with sugar flowers, sweets and butterflies.

Per slice
433 cals; 10g fat (of which 6g saturates);
87g carbohydrate; 0.3g salt

Dinosaur Cake

cuts into about 30 slices

Preparation: 1½ hours
Cooking time: about 45 minutes,
plus cooling, setting and drying

butter to grease
3 × 175g (6oz) butter quantity Madeira cake
mixture (see page 34)
1.5kg (3¼lb) buttercream (see page 48)
yellow, blue, black, purple, red and brown
(optional) food colouring pastes
white marzipan to model

You will also need

30.5cm (12 inch) round cake board
1 × 5mm (¼ inch) piping nozzle

tip

If you have any of the brighter green left
once you have piped the whole body,
then pipe on a thin line running from
the tip of the tail to the top of the head,
running along the centre of the
dinosaur body.

Per slice

569 cals; 30g fat (of which 18g saturates);
74g carbohydrate; 0.7g salt

1 Preheat the oven to 170°C (150°C fan oven) mark 3. Grease a 23cm (9 inch) round cake tin and line with greaseproof paper, then grease the paper lightly again. Do the same with a roasting tin, roughly 15 × 20.5cm (6 × 8 inches). Divide the Madeira cake mixture between the prepared tins, making sure that each tin is about half full. Bake for 1¾–2 hours or until the cakes are golden and a skewer inserted into the centre comes out clean. Leave the cakes to cool for 15 minutes in the tin, then transfer to a wire rack to cool completely.

2 When the cakes are completely cool, cut the round cake in half to make two semi-circles. Stand the two semi-circles side-by-side on their cut sides on the side of the cake board. This will form the body of the dinosaur.

3 Next, cut a 7.5cm (3 inch) wide strip off the entire length of one of the short edges of the rectangular cake. Cut this strip of cake in half horizontally down the middle to make two smaller cakes. Stack these cakes on top of one another to make the rough head, then carve with a knife to give the head a more realistic shape. Position the head a little way away from the body on the side of the board and bridge the body and the head with extra cake to make the neck. Use more of the rectangular cake to cut out the back leg shape and the wide part of the tail. Finally, use a knife to carve the back of the dinosaur down a little so that it meets the tail and neck well. Use some of these rounded trimmings to make the narrower end of the tail.

4 Once you are happy with the positioning of the carved dinosaur on the board, use some of the buttercream to sandwich the cake into position. If any gaps appear, then use trimmings to fill them up. Brush away any crumbs from the cake board.

5 Divide the remaining buttercream equally among three bowls. Using yellow and blue food colourings, colour the buttercream in two of the bowls green – making one a brighter green and one a darker, duller green. Add a touch of black (optional) to make both greens more reptilian. Now remove 2 tbsp buttercream from the remaining white buttercream bowl. Colour what is left in the bowl bright purple, then dull it down with a little black. Colour the reserved 2 tbsp buttercream red, cover and set aside.

6 Fit a 5mm (¼ inch) nozzle into a piping bag. Two-thirds fill the piping bag by dolloping in spoonfuls of alternating greens and purple (the marble effect will create a more realistic dinosaur skin). Or, if you like, pipe onto the cake in alternate colours, creating a striped effect.

7 Starting at the back of the dinosaur, pipe on the buttercream. You can either do neat beads, or join the beads together by not pulling the piping bag off completely before starting on the next bead. Cover the whole dinosaur in this way (filling the bag as before when needed). Leave to set for 30 minutes.

8 Next, mix together any remaining dark green and purple buttercream and spread roughly over the board. Swirl in a little of the reserved red buttercream. Next, colour a small amount of the marzipan black and a small amount brown. Roll all the black and brown out into circles, then roll out two white marzipan circles. Use to make the eyes. Alternatively, add a dot of red food colouring paste to make the eyes. Make large teeth with the undyed marzipan and stick on to the jaw.

9 Leave the dinosaur to dry for at least 3 hours before serving.

Jungle Cake

cuts into about 30 slices

To decorate: 1 hour, plus drying

20.5cm (8 inch) round chocolate, Madeira or Victoria Sponge cake (see pages 34 and 30)
12.5cm (5 inch) round chocolate, Madeira or Victoria Sponge cake
750g (1lb 10z) buttercream (see page 48)
blue, yellow, pink and black food colouring pastes
450g (1lb) white marzipan
cocoa powder, sifted
about 50g (2oz) each of pink and blue sugarpaste (optional)
icing sugar to dust

You will also need
cake board or plate

tip
Using marzipan to model animals will give them a more rounded, playful appearance – ideal for a child's birthday cake.

Per slice
368 cals; 19g fat (of which 11g saturates); 49g carbohydrate; 0.4g salt

1 Split both cakes in half horizontally and use some of the buttercream to sandwich them together. Use a little more buttercream to sandwich the smaller cake on to the larger cake, placing it off-centre. Place the cake on a cake board or plate.

2 Place two-thirds of the remaining buttercream in one bowl, and the remainder in a second bowl. Dye the larger amount of buttercream bright green, using blue and yellow food colouring, then set aside. Take a few tablespoonfuls of buttercream out of the smaller bowl and set aside. Dye the remaining icing in the second bowl bright blue and spread on to the cakes to resemble water cascading down from the top tier. Swirl in a little of the set-aside white buttercream to make the water look more realistic. Dye any remaining white buttercream bright pink and put into a small piping bag fitted with a small plain nozzle, then set aside. Spread the green buttercream over the cake, around the water. Swirl the icing as you go.

3 Using a little black food colouring paste, dye 125g (4oz) marzipan grey. Use most of this to make the drinking elephant: make an oval for the body and a round head, pinching out the trunk. Attach short sausage shapes for the legs and flattened ovals for the ears. Roll out two ovals from the white marzipan and attach one to each ear with a little water. Position the elephant on the lower tier, with its trunk in the water. Use a cocktail stick to prick two eyes and mark some stripes on the trunk. Use the remaining grey marzipan to make the hippo head: a fat oval with marked eyes, nostrils, mouth and snout. Attach two small ears to the top of the head. Dye a tiny amount of marzipan pink, roll out and attach to the ears. Position the hippo in the water on the top tier, securing the head at an angle on a little more grey marzipan.

4 Dye 40g (1½oz) of the remaining marzipan brown with cocoa powder. Set aside a small amount to make the spots on the giraffe. Use the remaining amount to make the monkey: an oval for the body and a round for the head, two longer sausages for the arms, and shorter sausages for the legs. Use a little uncoloured marzipan to put a flattened circle on the front of the stomach and a flattened oval on the bottom half of the face. Use a cocktail stick to mark out eyes and nostrils. Position on the base layer of the cake.

5 Dye 65g (2½oz) of the remaining marzipan yellow. Use a tiny bit to make a banana for the monkey to hold, and shape the rest into the sitting giraffe: a larger oval for the body and a round with a snout pinched out for the head. Attach two small triangles on top of the head for the ears, and use some of the reserved brown marzipan to make the horns. Shape and attach the legs. Stick on small dots of brown to give the giraffe his spots, and use a cocktail stick to mark the eyes and nostrils. Position on top of the cake, on the grass.

6 Dye a tiny bit of marzipan black for the alligator eyes. Reserve a tiny bit of uncoloured marzipan for the teeth. Dye the remaining marzipan green and shape some of it into the alligator heads. Add the eyes and teeth. Position the heads in the water and use a cocktail stick to make lines across the snouts. Lightly dust a work surface with icing sugar, then roll out any remaining green marzipan and cut out leaves – attach these where you want. Using the reserved pink buttercream, pipe pink rosette flowers around the cake. Alternatively, use pink and blue sugarpaste and a small plunger blossom cutter to cut out blossom shapes (see page 75) and attach these where you want. Leave to dry.

A Day at the Races

To decorate: 1 hour, plus drying

575g (1lb 4½oz) white sugarpaste
icing sugar, sifted, to dust
18cm (7 inch) round marzipanned fruit cake
brown and black food colouring paste
a little boiled and cooled water or brandy
green buttercream or thick glacé icing
to pipe

You will also need

23cm (9 inch) round cake board
cocktail stick
ribbon

tip

This clever cake uses the cake board to mimic the brim of a top hat.

1 Dye 50g (2oz) white sugarpaste brown, then use the majority of it to mould the horse's body. Decide which is to be the visible side of the horse, then shape the front two legs and one rear leg, tucking them under the horse body. Use the rest of the brown sugarpaste to shape the horse's head and neck, pinching out small ears when you have finished. Use a cocktail stick to make nostrils. Attach to the body using some pressure, then rub along the seam.

2 Dye 15g (½oz) white sugarpaste light brown, then pinch off a small bit and press out into a flattened strip, then place down the front of the horse's face. Lightly dust a work surface with icing sugar and roll out the remaining light brown icing thinly, then cut into thin strands for the mane. Dye 40g (1½oz) of the remaining white sugarpaste black. Roll out a little and cut into thin strands for the mane and two circles for the eyes, then shape the rest into the tail and saddle. Attach both light brown and black strands to the horse to make the mane, and the eyes to the head, then attach the saddle and tail.

3 Position the marzipanned cake in the centre of the cake board. Using a little of the black food colouring, dye 450g (1lb) sugarpaste grey.

4 Lightly dust a work surface with icing sugar and roll out the grey sugarpaste until it's large enough to cover the whole cake, cake board and the sides of the cake board. Brush the cake and cake board (remembering the sides of the board) with boiled and cooled water or brandy. Loosely roll the sugarpaste around a rolling pin and unroll into position on the cake. Smooth over the cake, working it carefully into position with your hands. Flatten on to the cake board and sides of the board. Trim the excess. To decorate the hat, you can either dye the trimmings black and roll out into a strip 2.5cm (1 inch) wide and long enough to wrap around the base of the cake plus a bow (secure both with a little boiled water or brandy), or use ribbon as shown.

5 Roll out the remaining white sugarpaste and cut into a rectangle. If you like, you can scallop or crimp the edges to give them interest. Secure on top of the hat, placing it off-centre.

6 Position the horse behind the plaque. Use a little green icing to pipe grass around the horse as well as a birthday message on the plaque. Leave to dry.

Per slice
323 cals; 10g fat (of which 4g saturates);
59g carbohydrate; 0.2g salt

cuts into about 16 slices

Preparation: 1½ hours
Cooking time: about 1 hour, plus cooling,
setting and drying

2 × baked marble cakes (see page 35)
500g (1lb 2oz) vanilla or chocolate
buttercream (see page 48)
icing sugar, sifted, to dust
about 800g (1lb 12oz) white sugarpaste
yellow (or gold) and black food colourings
gold lustre dust
silver balls (optional)

You will also need

1 × medium round cake board

tip

Use any design or colour you like to
transform this cake into a fashionista's
dream. Remember to always keep any
sugarpaste not in use covered with
clingfilm to stop it drying out.

1   Cut both cooled marble cakes in half horizontally. Put the narrow base section of one of the cakes on a cake board. Spread some buttercream over the top, then lay on the wider top, cut-side down. Ice the top of the reassembled cake with more buttercream. Next, lay on the wider top section of the other cake, cut side up. Spread over some more buttercream, then top with the remaining narrow base section, cut side down. Your large cake should have a slight diamond shape.

2   If you want, carve the cake into more of a handbag shape, then spread any remaining buttercream lightly over the cake and leave to set for 30 minutes.

3   Lightly dust a work surface with icing sugar and roll out 500g (1lb 2oz) white sugarpaste until it's large enough to cover the cake. With the help of the rolling pin, lift the icing on to the cake and smooth down. Trim any excess icing.

4   Next, tint 75g (3oz) white sugarpaste yellow (or as close to gold as you can get it). Roll out 50g (2oz) and cut into a strip about 25.5cm (10 inches) long and 2.5cm (1 inch) wide. Use a knife, cocktail stick or crimpers to mark a zip pattern along the centre of the strip and stitch marks along the edges. Brush the strip with gold lustre dust. Add the trimmings to the remaining yellow sugarpaste and roll into one large and one small rectangle, to make the clasp, and four small squares, to make the handle fastenings. Use a knife, cocktail stick or crimpers to mark stitch marks around the squares. Brush with gold lustre. Reroll the trimmings into piping for the flap. Put all to one side.

5   Dye the remaining sugarpaste black. Attach the zip to the top of the cake with a little boiled and cooled water. Shape a little of the black sugarpaste into two small triangles or rectangles and fix one to each end of the zip, using water and pressure. If you like, press some silver balls on to the black ends of the zip for added glitz.

6   Lightly dust a work surface with icing sugar and roll out some more of the black sugarpaste until it is about 5mm (¼ inch) thick. Cut into a rounded, tapered square to make the closing flap. Using a knife, cocktail stick or crimpers, add some marks around the edges to look like stitching, then lay the flap over the centre of the zip. Fix the two gold rectangles in place to make the clasp, using water and pressure. If you like, add silver balls to the clasp as rivets.

7   Roll out the remaining black sugarpaste and cut out two strips for the handles. Place over the flap and secure each end with a yellow square handle fastening. If you like, press a silver ball into the middle of each square. Attach the yellow piping to the flap, using water and pressure.

8   Roll out the black sugarpaste trimmings thinly and cut out zebra-pattern shapes. Brush them with lustre dust, if you like, and fix to the cake with a little water. Leave to dry before serving.

Per slice
686 cals; 32g fat (of which 17g saturates);
101g carbohydrate; 0.9g salt

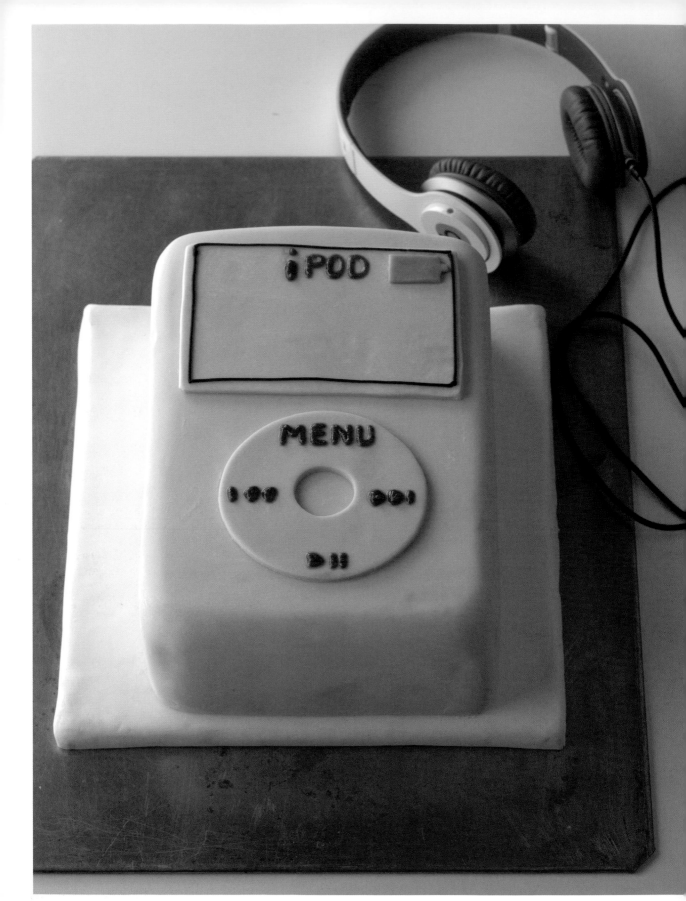

iPod Cake

cuts into about 25 slices

Preparation: 1½ hours
Cooking time: about 1 hour, plus cooling, setting and drying

unsalted butter to grease
2 × 175g (6oz) butter quantity Madeira cake mixture (see page 34)
icing sugar, sifted, to dust
about 825g (1lb 13oz) white sugarpaste (about 100g/3½oz less if you are not decorating the base of the cake with a metallic strip)
a little thick glacé icing to pipe
black, blue and green (optional) food colouring pastes
500g (1lb 2oz) chocolate buttercream (see page 48)
metallic lustre dust (optional)

You will also need
large rectangular cake board
small greaseproof piping bag (see page 58)

tip
This simple and effective design combines to make a cake that any music or gadget-lover will adore – and it can be sliced easily. Remember to always keep any sugarpaste not in use covered with clingfilm to stop it drying out.

1 Preheat the oven to 170°C (150°C fan oven) mark 3. Grease a roasting tin roughly 35 x 26 x 4.5cm (13½ x 10 x 1¾ inches) and line with greaseproof paper, then grease the paper lightly. Make the Madeira cake mixture and spoon into the prepared tin. Level the surface and bake until golden on top and a skewer inserted into the centre comes out clean, about 1 hour. Leave to cool for 15 minutes, then lift out of the tin (using the greaseproof paper) and leave to cool completely on a wire rack.

2 Meanwhile, lightly dust a work surface with icing sugar, then roll out 75g (3oz) white sugarpaste until it's large enough to cut out a 9 x 12.5cm (3½ × 5 inch) rectangle. Move the rectangle on to baking parchment to dry. Next, roll out 100g (3½oz) white sugarpaste and cut out a 10cm (4 inch) circle with a cutter. Transfer the circle to the baking parchment, then cut out a 5cm (2 inch) hole in the middle.

3 Dye the thick glacé icing grey or black, then use to half-fill a small greaseproof piping bag. Snip the tip of the bag and pipe the iPod logo and, if you like, either a birthday message or a list of settings (such as artists, music, photographs) on to the plaque (dried rectangle). If you like, dye a very small amount of the sugarpaste green, roll it out, cut into the shape of a battery and add to the plaque. Pipe symbols for play, pause, fast-forward and rewind on to each quarter of the circle. Leave to dry.

4 Cut the cooled cake in half horizontally. Put the bottom half on a large cake board and spread the top with some of the buttercream. Top with the other cake half, then spread the remaining buttercream lightly over the top and sides of the cake. Leave to set for 30 minutes.

5 Meanwhile, dye 550g (1lb 4oz) white sugarpaste a bright blue. Wrap well in clingfilm. If you like, you can make a grey metallic strip to go round the base of the cake – using a little of the black food colouring, dye the remaining 100g (3½oz) white sugarpaste grey. Wrap well in clingfilm.

6 Lightly dust a work surface with icing sugar and roll out the blue sugarpaste until it's large enough to cover the top and sides of the cake. Roll the icing gently around the rolling pin, then lift on to the cake. Use your hands to smooth into place, and trim any excess at the base of the cake. Using a dry paintbrush, brush metallic lustre over the cake, if you like.

7 If you are making the base strip, roll out the reserved grey icing until it is about 5mm (¼ inch) thick, then cut into 4 x 2.5cm (1 inch) wide strips, each measured to one side of the cake, or measure the circumference of the cake and cut one long strip. Brush the strip(s) with metallic lustre, then fix to the cake with a little water. Finally, fix the plaque and circle in place with a little water and leave to dry.

Per slice
457 cals; 18g fat (of which 11g saturates);
74g carbohydrate; 0.5g salt

Football Cake

cuts into about 30 slices

Preparation: 1½ hours
Cooking time: about 1½ hours,
plus cooling and drying

225g (8oz) unsalted butter, softened,
plus extra to grease
3 × 175g (6oz) unsalted butter quantity
Chocolate Victoria Sponge mixture
(see page 30)
3 tbsp cocoa powder, sifted
525g (1lb 3oz) icing sugar, sifted,
plus extra to dust
1–3 tbsp milk, as needed
1kg (2¼ lb) white sugarpaste
black and red food colouring pastes
black royal icing (optional, see page 43), to
pipe

You will also need

25.5cm (10 inch) round cake board
5cm (2 inch) hexagon template (see page 63)
fine paintbrush

tip

The only choice of cake for the ultimate
football fan. If you like, personalise the
scarf of this cake to match the team of
your choice.

1 Preheat the oven to 190°C (170°C fan oven) mark 5. Grease a 23cm (9 inch) round cake tin and line with greaseproof paper, then lightly grease the paper again. Make the chocolate Victoria sponge mixture following the method on page 28.

2 Empty the cake mixture into the prepared tin and bake for 1½ hours or until a skewer inserted into the centre comes out clean. Leave to cool for 15 minutes in the tin, then take out of the tin and cool completely on a wire rack.

3 When the cake has cooled completely, make the buttercream. Blend the cocoa powder with 2 tbsp boiling water to make a smooth paste, then set aside to cool. Next, put the butter into a large bowl and, using a hand-held electric whisk, beat until light and smooth. Gradually beat in the icing sugar, followed by the cooled cocoa butter mixture. Add the milk, if needed, to make a smooth and spreadable icing.

4 Split the cake horizontally into three even layers, then sandwich the layers back together with some of the buttercream. Put the cake on a cake board of the same size, then spread the remaining buttercream thinly over the top and sides of the cake and the sides of the cake board. Set aside to dry for 30 minutes.

5 Lightly dust a worksurface with icing sugar and roll out 650g (1lb 7oz) of the white sugarpaste, then use to cover the top and sides of the cake and cake board. Smooth all over with a cake smoother or hands dusted in icing sugar.

6 Next, dye about 65g (2½oz) of the remaining sugarpaste black, and roll out as before. Using a 5cm (2 inch) diameter hexagon template, cut out seven black hexagons. Using a little water, stick a hexagon in the centre on top of the cake. Position the paper template next to one side of the central hexagon and, using a fine paintbrush dipped in the black food colouring paste, paint around the sides. Alternatively pipe a black thin line. Continue moving the template around the central hexagon, painting/piping in the edges to mark the seams of the football. Using the painted hexagons as a guide, stick on the remaining black hexagons. Paint/pipe in any missing seams.

7 Dye the remaining sugarpaste red, then roll out as above into a long strip. The strip needs to be wide enough to cover the sides of the cake and board and long enough to wrap round the cake with a little excess. You can add a pattern to the strip if you like, by rolling over it with a textured (basketweave) rolling pin. Trim to neaten, then lightly roll up from one of the short ends. Brush the sides of the cake with water and unwrap the red strip on to it, pressing lightly to stick. Trim the overlapping short end to give the scarf a fringe.

8 If you like, using royal icing, pipe a birthday message or the name of your chosen team on to the scarf and leave to dry.

Per slice
529 cals; 23g fat (of which 14g saturates);
82g carbohydrate; 0.7g salt

Cupcakes

Fairy Cakes

makes 18

Preparation: 20 minutes
Cooking time: 10–15 minutes,
plus cooling and setting

125g (4oz) self-raising flour, sifted
1 tsp baking powder
125g (4oz) caster sugar
125g (4oz) unsalted butter, very soft
2 medium eggs
1 tbsp milk

For the icing and decoration
225g (8oz) icing sugar, sifted
assorted food colourings (optional)
sweets, sprinkles or coloured sugar

1 Preheat the oven to 200°C (180°C fan oven) mark 6. Put paper cases into 18 of the holes in two bun tins.
2 Put the flour, baking powder, sugar, butter, eggs and milk into a mixing bowl and beat with a hand-held electric whisk for 2 minutes or until the mixture is pale and very soft. Half-fill each paper case with the mixture.
3 Bake for 10–15 minutes until golden brown. Transfer to a wire rack and leave to cool completely.
4 Put the icing sugar into a bowl and gradually blend in 2–3 tbsp warm water until the icing is fairly stiff, but spreadable. Add a couple of drops of food colouring, if you like.
5 When the cakes are cold, spread the tops with the icing and decorate. Leave to set.

variation

CHOCOLATE FAIRY CAKES Replace 2 tbsp of the flour with the same amount of cocoa powder. Stir 50g (2oz) chocolate drops, sultanas or chopped dried apricots into the mixture at the end of step 1. Complete the recipe.

Per cake
160 cals; 6g fat (of which 4g saturates);
26g carbohydrate; 0.2g salt

Chocolate Cupcakes

makes 18

Preparation: 15 minutes
**Cooking time: 20 minutes, plus cooling
and setting**

125g (4oz) unsalted butter, softened
125g (4oz) light muscovado sugar
2 medium eggs, beaten
15g (½oz) cocoa powder
100g (3½oz) self-raising flour
100g (3½oz) plain chocolate (at least 70%
cocoa solids), roughly chopped

For the topping
150ml (¼ pint) double cream
100g (3½oz) plain chocolate (at least 70%
cocoa solids), broken up

1 Preheat the oven to 190°C (170°C fan oven) mark 5. Line a 12-hole and a 6-hole bun tin or muffin tin with paper muffin cases.
2 Beat the butter and sugar together until light and fluffy. Gradually beat in the eggs. Sift the cocoa powder with the flour and fold into the creamed mixture with the chopped chocolate. Divide the mixture among the paper cases and lightly flatten the surface with the back of a spoon.
3 Bake for 20 minutes, then transfer to a wire rack and leave to cool completely.
4 For the topping, put the cream and chocolate into a heavy-based pan over a low heat and heat until melted, then allow to cool and thicken slightly. Spoon on to the cooled cakes, then stand the cakes upright on the wire rack and leave for 30 minutes to set.

Per cupcake
203 cals; 14g fat (of which 8g saturates);
19g carbohydrate; 0.2g salt

Cherry Bakewell Cupcakes

makes 12

Preparation: 30 minutes, plus chilling
**Cooking time: 25 minutes, plus cooling
and setting**

175g (6oz) unsalted butter, softened

175g (6oz) caster sugar

3 medium eggs

150g (5oz) self-raising flour, sifted

1 tsp baking powder

75g (3oz) ground almonds

1 tsp almond extract

75g (3oz) glacé cherries, finely chopped

For the topping and decoration

1 tbsp custard powder

100ml (3½fl oz) milk

50g (2oz) unsalted butter, softened

250g (9oz) icing sugar, sifted

red sugar sprinkles

1 Preheat the oven to 190°C (170°C fan oven) mark 5. Line a 12-hole muffin tin with paper muffin cases.

2 Using a hand-held electric whisk, whisk the butter and caster sugar in a bowl, or beat with a wooden spoon, until pale and creamy. Gradually whisk in the eggs until just combined. Using a metal spoon, fold in the flour, baking powder, ground almonds, almond extract and cherries until combined. Divide the mixture equally among the paper cases.

3 Bake for 20 minutes or until golden and risen. Cool in the tin for 5 minutes, then transfer to a wire rack and leave to cool completely.

4 For the topping, put the custard powder into a jug and add a little of the milk to make a smooth paste. Put the remaining milk into a pan and bring just to the boil. Pour the hot milk on to the custard paste and stir. Return to the milk pan and heat gently for 1–2 minutes until it thickens. Remove from the heat, cover with dampened greaseproof paper to prevent a skin forming and cool completely.

5 Put the custard into a bowl and, using a hand-held electric whisk, whisk in the butter. Chill for 30 minutes.

6 Gradually whisk the icing sugar into the chilled custard mixture until you have a smooth, thick icing. Using a small palette knife, spread a little custard cream over the top of each cake, then decorate with sugar sprinkles. Stand the cakes upright on the wire rack and leave for about 1 hour to set.

Per cupcake
405 cals; 21g fat (of which 11g saturates);
53g carbohydrate; 0.4g salt

Marbled Chocolate Cupcakes

makes 12

Preparation: 40 minutes

Cooking time: 20 minutes, plus cooling

75g (3oz) unsalted butter, softened

150g (5oz) caster sugar

2 medium eggs

25g (1oz) self-raising flour, sifted

125g (4oz) plain flour, sifted

½ tsp bicarbonate of soda

2 tsp vanilla extract

150ml (¼ pint) buttermilk

25g (1oz) cocoa powder, sifted

For the icing

125g (4oz) unsalted butter, softened

350g (12oz) icing sugar, sifted

2 tsp vanilla extract

2 tbsp cocoa powder, sifted

1 Preheat the oven to 190°C (170°C fan oven), mark 5. Line a 12-hole muffin tin with paper muffin cases.

2 Using a hand-held electric whisk, whisk the butter and caster sugar in a bowl, or beat with a wooden spoon, until pale and creamy. Gradually whisk in the eggs until just combined. Using a metal spoon, fold in both flours, the bicarbonate of soda, vanilla extract and buttermilk until combined. Put half this mixture into another bowl and whisk in the cocoa powder. Then very lightly fold this mixture into the vanilla mixture, to create a marbled effect. Divide the mixture equally among the paper cases.

3 Bake for 20 minutes or until golden and risen. Leave to cool in the tin for 5 minutes, then transfer to a wire rack to cool completely.

4 For the topping, put the butter into a bowl and whisk until fluffy. Gradually whisk in half the icing sugar, then add the vanilla extract, 2 tbsp boiling water and the remaining icing sugar and whisk until light and fluffy. Put half the mixture into another bowl and whisk in the cocoa powder.

5 Insert a star nozzle into a piping bag, then fill the bag alternately with the vanilla and chocolate buttercreams. Pipe a swirl on to the top of each cake.

Per cupcake

360 cals; 16g fat (of which 10g saturates);
54g carbohydrate; 0.5g salt

Raspberry Ripple Cupcakes

makes 9

Preparation: 30 minutes
Cooking time: 20 minutes, plus cooling

50g (2oz) seedless raspberry jam
50g (2oz) fresh raspberries
125g (4oz) unsalted butter, softened
100g (3½oz) caster sugar
2 medium eggs
1 tbsp milk
150g (5oz) self-raising flour, sifted

For the topping and decoration
150g (5oz) fresh raspberries
300ml (½ pint) whipping cream
50g (2oz) icing sugar, sifted

1 Preheat the oven to 190°C (170°C fan oven) mark 5. Line a 12-hole muffin tin with 9 paper muffin cases.
2 Mix the raspberry jam with the 50g (2oz) raspberries, lightly crushing the raspberries. Set aside.
3 Using a hand-held electric whisk, whisk the butter and caster sugar in a bowl, or beat with a wooden spoon, until pale and creamy. Gradually whisk in the eggs and milk until just combined. Using a metal spoon, fold in the flour until just combined, then carefully fold in the raspberry jam mixture until just marbled, being careful not to over-mix. Divide the mixture equally among the paper cases.
4 Bake for 20 minutes or until golden and risen. Cool in the tin for 5 minutes, then transfer to a wire rack and leave to cool completely.
5 For the decoration, reserve 9 raspberries. Mash the remaining raspberries in a bowl with a fork. Pass through a sieve into a bowl to remove the seeds. Using a hand-held electric whisk, whip the cream and icing sugar together until stiff peaks form. Mix the raspberry purée into the cream until combined.
6 Insert a star nozzle into a piping bag, then fill the bag with the cream and pipe a swirl on to the top of each cake. Decorate each with a raspberry.

Per cupcake
385 cals; 26g fat (of which 16g saturates);
36g carbohydrate; 0.5g salt

makes 6

Preparation: 30 minutes
Cooking time: 25 minutes,
plus cooling and setting

2 medium eggs
75g (3oz) caster sugar
150ml (¼ pint) sunflower oil
150g (5oz) plain flour, sifted
½ tsp baking powder
1 tsp vanilla extract
15g (½oz) Rice Krispies

For the topping and decoration
100g (3½oz) white chocolate, broken into
pieces
15g (½oz) unsalted butter
25g (1oz) Rice Krispies
12 chocolate mini eggs

1 Preheat the oven to 180°C (160°C fan oven), mark 4. Line a 6-hole muffin tin with paper muffin cases.
2 Separate the eggs, putting the whites in a clean, greasefree bowl and the yolks in another. Add the sugar to the yolks and whisk with a hand-held electric whisk until pale and creamy. Then whisk in the oil until combined.
3 Whisk the egg whites until soft peaks form. Using a metal spoon, quickly fold the flour, baking powder, vanilla extract and Rice Krispies into the egg yolk mixture until just combined. Add half the egg whites to the egg yolk mixture to loosen, then carefully fold in the remaining egg whites. Divide the mixture equally among the paper cases.
4 Bake for 20–25 minutes until golden and risen. Leave to cool in the tin for 5 minutes, then transfer to a wire rack to cool completely.
5 For the topping, put the chocolate and butter into a heatproof bowl and place over a pan of barely simmering water, making sure the base of the bowl doesn't touch the water. Gently heat until the chocolate has melted, stirring occasionally until smooth. Remove the bowl from the heat, add the Rice Krispies and fold through until coated. Spoon the mixture on top of each cake, pressing down lightly, then top each with 2 chocolate eggs. Stand the cakes upright on the wire rack and leave for about 1 hour to set.

Per cupcake
378 cals; 27g fat (of which 8 g saturates);
32g carbohydrate; 0.2g salt

The Ultimate Carrot Cupcakes

makes 12

Preparation: 30 minutes
Cooking time: 20 minutes, plus cooling

150g (5oz) carrots, peeled
50g (2oz) raisins
175g (6oz) self-raising flour, sifted
½ tsp bicarbonate of soda
150g (5oz) light soft brown sugar
zest of 1 orange
½ tsp ground mixed spice
3 medium eggs
100ml (3½fl oz) sunflower oil
75ml (2½fl oz) buttermilk

For the topping and decoration
50g (2oz) icing sugar, sifted
250g (9oz) mascarpone cheese
100g (3½oz) quark cheese
juice of ½ orange
red, yellow and green sugarpaste (optional)

1 Preheat the oven to 190°C (170°C fan oven) mark 5. Line a 12-hole muffin tin with paper muffin cases.
2 Coarsely grate the carrots and put into a large bowl. Add the raisins, flour, bicarbonate of soda, brown sugar, orange zest and mixed spice. Put the eggs, oil and buttermilk into a jug and lightly beat together until combined. Pour the egg mixture into the flour and stir with a spatula until just combined. Divide the mixture equally among the paper cases.
3 Bake for 20 minutes or until lightly golden and risen. Cool in the tin for 5 minutes, then transfer to a wire rack and leave to cool completely.
4 For the topping, mix the icing sugar with the mascarpone, quark and orange juice to a smooth icing. Using a small palette knife, spread a little of the icing over each cake. Use the coloured sugarpaste to make small carrots, if you like, and decorate the cakes with them.

Per cupcake
255 cals; 12g fat (of which 4g saturates);
34g carbohydrate; 0.3g salt

Lavender and Honey Cupcakes

makes 9

Preparation: 35 minutes
Cooking time: 15–20 minutes,
plus cooling and setting

125g (4oz) unsalted butter, softened
125g (4oz) clear honey
2 medium eggs
125g (4oz) self-raising flour, sifted
1 tsp baking powder

For the icing and decoration
3 honey and lavender tea bags
2 tsp unsalted butter
250g (9oz) icing sugar, sifted
red and blue food colouring
purple sugar stars
edible silver dust (optional)

1 Preheat the oven to 190°C (170°C fan oven) mark 5. Line a 12-hole muffin tin with 9 paper muffin cases.
2 Using a hand-held electric whisk, whisk the butter and honey in a bowl, or beat with a wooden spoon, until combined. Gradually whisk in the eggs until just combined. Using a metal spoon, fold in the flour and baking powder until combined. Divide the mixture equally among the paper cases.
3 Bake for 15–20 minutes until golden and risen. Cool in the tin for 5 minutes, then transfer to a wire rack and leave to cool completely.
4 For the icing, infuse the tea bags in 50ml (2fl oz) boiling water in a small bowl for 5 minutes. Remove the tea bags and squeeze out the excess water into the bowl. Stir in the butter until melted. Put the icing sugar into a large bowl, add the infused tea mixture and stir to make a smooth icing. Add a few drops of red and blue food colouring until it is lilac in colour.
5 Spoon a little icing on top of each cake, to flood the tops, then sprinkle with stars. Stand the cakes upright on the wire rack and leave for about 1 hour to set. Dust with edible dust, if you like, when set.

Per cupcake
316 cals; 13g fat (of which 8g saturates);
50g carbohydrate; 0.3g salt

Mini Green Tea Cupcakes

makes 12

Preparation: 40 minutes, plus infusing
Cooking time: 25 minutes, plus cooling

100ml (3½fl oz) milk
2 tsp loose green tea leaves
100g (3½oz) unsalted butter, softened
125g (4oz) caster sugar
2 medium eggs
150g (5oz) self-raising flour, sifted
½ tsp baking powder

For the topping and decoration
3 tsp loose green tea leaves
about 75ml (2½fl oz) boiling water
75g (3oz) unsalted butter, softened
250g (9oz) icing sugar, sifted
ready-made sugar flowers

1 Preheat the oven to 190°C (170°C fan oven) mark 5. Line a 12-hole muffin tin with paper fairy cake or bun cases.

2 Put the milk into a small pan and bring to the boil. Add the green tea leaves and leave to infuse for 30 minutes.

3 Using a hand-held electric whisk, whisk the butter and caster sugar in a bowl, or beat with a wooden spoon, until pale and creamy. Gradually whisk in the eggs until just combined. Pass the green tea milk through a sieve into the bowl, then discard the tea. Using a metal spoon, fold in the flour and baking powder until combined. Divide the mixture equally among the paper cases.

4 Bake for 18–20 minutes until golden and risen. Cool in the tin for 5 minutes, then transfer to a wire rack and leave to cool completely.

5 For the topping, put the green tea leaves into a jug, add about 75ml (2½fl oz) boiling water and leave to infuse for 5 minutes.

6 Put the butter into a bowl and whisk until fluffy. Gradually add the icing sugar and whisk until combined. Pass the green tea through a sieve into the bowl, then discard the tea. Continue to whisk until light and fluffy.

7 Insert a star nozzle into a piping bag, then fill the bag with the buttercream and pipe a swirl on to the top of each cake. Decorate each with a sugar flower.

Per cupcake
282 cals; 13g fat (of which 8g saturates);
41g carbohydrate; 0.3g salt

Pink Cupcakes

Preparation: 35 minutes
Cooking time: 20 minutes, plus cooling

150g (5oz) raw beetroot, peeled and finely
grated
200g (7oz) self-raising flour, sifted
½ tsp bicarbonate of soda
150g (5oz) caster sugar
zest of 1 orange
2 medium eggs
100ml (3½fl oz) sunflower oil
125ml (4fl oz) buttermilk

For the topping and decoration
100g (3½ oz) unsalted butter, softened
350g (12oz) icing sugar, sifted
50ml (2fl oz) milk
pink food colouring
ready-made pink or red sugar flowers
(optional)

1 Preheat the oven to 190°C (170°C fan oven) mark 5. Line a 12-hole muffin tin with paper muffin cases.
2 Put the beetroot, flour, bicarbonate of soda, caster sugar and orange zest into a bowl. Put the eggs, oil and buttermilk into a jug and lightly beat together until combined. Pour the egg mixture into the flour and stir with a spatula until just combined. Divide the mixture equally among the paper cases.
3 Bake for 20 minutes or until lightly golden and risen. Cool in the tin for 5 minutes, then transfer to a wire rack and leave to cool completely.
4 For the topping, put the butter into a bowl and whisk until fluffy. Gradually whisk in half the icing sugar, then add the milk, a little pink food colouring and the remaining icing sugar, and whisk until light and fluffy.
5 Insert a star nozzle into a piping bag, then fill the bag with the buttercream and pipe small swirls all the way around the top of each cake. Decorate with the sugar flowers, if you like.

Per cupcake
361 cals; 14g fat (of which 6g saturates);
58g carbohydrate; 0.2g salt

Coconut and Lime Cupcakes

makes 12

Preparation: 30 minutes
Cooking time: 18–20 minutes,
plus cooling and setting

275g (10oz) plain flour, sifted
1 tbsp baking powder
100g (3½oz) caster sugar
zest of 1 lime
50g (2oz) desiccated coconut
2 medium eggs
100ml (3½fl oz) sunflower oil
225ml (8fl oz) natural yogurt
50ml (2fl oz) milk

For the topping
150g (5oz) icing sugar, sifted
juice of 1 lime
1–2 tsp boiling water
50g (2oz) desiccated coconut

1 Preheat the oven to 200°C (180°C fan oven) mark 6. Line a 12-hole muffin tin with paper muffin cases.
2 Put the flour, baking powder, caster sugar, lime zest and coconut into a large bowl. Put the eggs, oil, yogurt and milk into a jug and lightly beat together until combined. Pour the yogurt mixture into the flour and stir with a spatula until just combined. Divide the mixture equally among the paper cases.
3 Bake for 18–20 minutes until lightly golden and risen. Cool in the tin for 5 minutes, then transfer to a wire rack and leave to cool completely.
4 For the decoration, mix the icing sugar with the lime juice and enough boiling water to make a thick, smooth icing. Put the coconut into a shallow bowl. Dip each cake top into the icing until coated, allowing the excess to drip off, then carefully dip into the coconut until coated. Stand the cakes upright on the wire rack and leave for about 1 hour to set.

Per cupcake
291 cals; 13g fat (of which 6g saturates);
42g carbohydrate; 0.1g salt

Honeycomb Cream Cupcakes

makes 9

Preparation: 30 minutes
Cooking time: 20 minutes, plus cooling

125g (4oz) unsalted butter, softened
50g (2oz) caster sugar
2 medium eggs
75g (3oz) clear honey
125g (4oz) self-raising flour, sifted
50g (2oz) rolled oats
½ tsp baking powder
1 tbsp milk

For the topping and decoration
125g (4oz) unsalted butter, softened
300g (11oz) golden icing sugar, sifted
2 tbsp milk
1 Crunchie bar, thinly sliced

1   Preheat the oven to 190°C (170°C fan oven) mark 5. Line a 12-hole muffin tin with 9 paper muffin cases.
2   Using a hand-held electric whisk, whisk the butter and caster sugar in a bowl, or beat with a wooden spoon, until pale and creamy. Gradually whisk in the eggs and honey until just combined. Using a metal spoon, fold in the flour, oats, baking powder and milk until combined. Divide the mixture equally among the paper cases.
3   Bake for 20 minutes or until golden and risen. Cool in the tin for 5 minutes, then transfer to a wire rack and leave to cool completely.
4   For the topping, put the butter into a bowl and whisk until fluffy. Gradually whisk in half the icing sugar, then add the milk and the remaining icing sugar and whisk until light and fluffy.
5   Insert a star nozzle into a piping bag, then fill the bag with the buttercream and pipe a swirl on to the top of each cake. When ready to serve, decorate each with a few slices of Crunchie.

Per cupcake
480 cals; 25g fat (of which 15g saturates);
65g carbohydrate; 0.6g salt

Banoffee Cupcakes

makes 12

Preparation: 30 minutes
Cooking time: 20 minutes, plus cooling

175g (6oz) self-raising flour, sifted
½ tsp bicarbonate of soda
150g (5oz) light soft brown sugar
1 banana (about 150g/5oz), peeled
3 medium eggs
100g (3½oz) unsalted butter, melted
75ml (2½fl oz) buttermilk

For the topping and decoration
150g (5oz) dulce de leche toffee sauce
75g (3oz) unsalted butter, softened
250g (9oz) golden icing sugar, sifted
mini fudge chunks (optional)

1 Preheat the oven to 190°C (170°C fan oven) mark 5. Line a 12-hole muffin tin with paper muffin cases.
2 Put the flour, bicarbonate of soda and brown sugar into a large bowl. Mash the banana with a fork in a small bowl. Put the eggs, melted butter and buttermilk into a jug and lightly beat together until combined. Pour into the flour mixture along with the mashed banana and stir with a spatula until just combined. Divide the mixture equally among the paper cases.
3 Bake for 18–20 minutes until lightly golden and risen. Cool in the tin for 5 minutes, then transfer to a wire rack and leave to cool completely.
4 For the decoration, whisk together the dulce de leche and butter in a bowl until combined. Gradually whisk in the icing sugar until light and fluffy. Use a palette knife to spread the buttercream on to the top of each cake. Decorate with the mini fudge chunks, if you like.

Per cupcake
404 cals; 16g fat (of which 10g saturates);
63g carbohydrate; 0.4g salt

Cookies and Cream Cupcakes

makes 12

Preparation: 30 minutes
Cooking time: 15–20 minutes, plus cooling

75g (3oz) mini Oreo cookies
175g (6oz) unsalted butter, softened
150g (5oz) caster sugar
3 medium eggs
175g (6oz) self-raising flour, sifted
½ tsp baking powder
3 tbsp milk
½ tsp vanilla extract

For the icing
75g (3oz) unsalted butter, softened
150g (5oz) icing sugar, sifted
2 tsp vanilla extract
1 tsp cocoa powder

1 Preheat the oven to 200°C (180°C fan oven), mark 6. Line a 12-hole muffin tin with paper muffin cases. Reserve 12 mini cookies and roughly chop the remainder.
2 Using a hand-held electric whisk, whisk the butter and caster sugar in a bowl (or beat with a wooden spoon) until pale and creamy. Gradually whisk in the eggs until just combined. Using a metal spoon, fold in the flour, baking powder, milk, vanilla extract and chopped cookies until combined. Divide the mixture equally among the paper cases.
3 Bake for 15–20 minutes until golden and risen. Leave to cool in the tin for 5 minutes, then transfer to a wire rack to cool completely.
4 For the decoration, put the butter into a bowl and whisk until fluffy. Gradually add the icing sugar and vanilla extract and whisk until light and fluffy. Using a small palette knife, spread the buttercream over the top of each cake. Sift a little cocoa powder on to the top of each cake and then decorate each with a reserved Oreo cookie.

Per cupcake
357 cals; 21g fat (of which 13g saturates);
41g carbohydrate; 0.5g salt

Pistachio and Polenta Cupcakes

makes 12

Preparation: 35 minutes
Cooking time: 25 minutes, plus cooling

150g (5oz) shelled pistachio nuts
175g (6oz) unsalted butter, softened
175g (6oz) caster sugar
3 medium eggs
200g (7oz) fine polenta
½ tsp baking powder
150g (5oz) ground almonds
zest of 2 lemons
2 tbsp milk

For the icing

75g (3oz) unsalted butter, softened
300g (11oz) icing sugar, sifted
juice of 2 lemons

1   Preheat the oven to 180°C (160°C fan oven) mark 4. Line a 12-hole muffin tin with paper muffin cases.
2   Whiz the pistachio nuts in a food processor until really finely chopped.
3   Using a hand-held electric whisk, whisk the butter and caster sugar in a bowl, or beat with a wooden spoon, until pale and creamy. Gradually whisk in the eggs until just combined. Using a metal spoon, fold in the polenta, baking powder, ground almonds, lemon zest, milk and 100g (3½oz) ground pistachio nuts until combined. Divide the mixture equally among the paper cases.
4   Bake for 25 minutes or until golden and risen. Cool in the tin for 5 minutes, then transfer to a wire rack and leave to cool completely.
5   For the icing, put the butter into a bowl and whisk until fluffy. Gradually whisk in half the icing sugar, then add the lemon juice and the remaining icing sugar, whisking until light and fluffy. Using a small palette knife, spread a little of the buttercream over the top of each cake, then sprinkle each with a little of the remaining chopped pistachio nuts.

Per cupcake
542 cals; 33g fat (of which 13g saturates);
56g carbohydrate; 0.6g salt

Sticky Gingerbread Cupcakes

Preparation: 35 minutes
Cooking time: 20 minutes, plus cooling

175g (6oz) self-raising flour

75g (3oz) unsalted butter, chilled and cut into cubes

¼ tsp bicarbonate of soda

2 tsp ground ginger

25g (1oz) stem ginger in syrup, finely chopped, plus 3 tbsp syrup from the jar

50g (2oz) dark muscovado sugar

50g (2oz) golden syrup

50g (2oz) treacle

juice of 1 orange

2 medium eggs, beaten

For the icing and decoration
100g (3½oz) unsalted butter, softened
200g (7oz) icing sugar, sifted
3 tbsp syrup from the stem ginger jar
1 tsp ground ginger
ready-made sugar flowers (optional)

1   Preheat the oven to 190°C (170°C fan oven), mark 5. Line a 12-hole muffin tin with 9 paper muffin cases.

2   Put the flour into a large bowl and, using your fingertips, rub in the butter until it resembles breadcrumbs. Stir in the bicarbonate of soda, ground ginger and stem ginger and set aside. Put the muscovado sugar, golden syrup, treacle and orange juice into a small pan and heat gently until the sugar dissolves. Leave to cool for 5 minutes.

3   Mix the eggs and warm sugar mixture into the flour mixture and stir with a spatula until just combined. Divide equally among the paper cases.

4   Bake for 20 minutes or until golden and risen. Remove from the oven and drizzle each cake with 1 tsp ginger syrup. Leave to cool in the tin for 5 minutes, then transfer to a wire rack to cool completely.

5   For the buttercream topping, put the butter into a bowl and whisk until fluffy. Add the icing sugar, ginger syrup and ground ginger. Whisk until light and fluffy. Using a small palette knife, spread a little buttercream over the top of each cake. Decorate with sugar flowers, if you like

Per cupcake
386 cals; 17g fat (of which 11g saturates);
58g carbohydrate; 0.5g salt

Be Mine Cupcakes

makes 12

Preparation: 30 minutes
Cooking time: 15 minutes, plus cooling

125g (4oz) unsalted butter, softened
100g (3½oz) caster sugar
2 medium eggs
125g (4oz) self-raising flour, sifted
½ tsp baking powder
1 × 51g bar Turkish Delight, finely chopped
1 tbsp rosewater

For the icing and decoration
75g (3oz) unsalted butter, softened
250g (9oz) icing sugar, sifted
2 tbsp rose water
pink and white heart-shaped sugar sprinkles
about 12 Loveheart sweets (optional)

1 Preheat the oven to 190°C (170°C fan oven), mark 5. Line a 12-hole muffin tin with paper cake cases.
2 Using a hand-held electric whisk, whisk the butter and caster sugar in a bowl, or beat with a wooden spoon, until pale and creamy. Gradually whisk in the eggs until just combined. Using a metal spoon, fold in the flour, baking powder, Turkish Delight and rose water until combined. Divide the mixture equally between the paper cases.
3 Bake for 15 minutes or until golden and risen. Leave to cool in the tin for 5 minutes, then transfer to a wire rack to cool completely.
4 For the topping, put the butter into a bowl and whisk until fluffy. Add the icing sugar and rose water and whisk until light and fluffy. Using a small palette knife, spread a little buttercream over the top of each cake. Decorate with sugar hearts, then top each with a Loveheart, if you like.

Per cupcake
289 cals; 15g fat (of which 9g saturates);
40g carbohydrate; 0.3g salt

Secret Garden Cupcakes

makes 12

Preparation: 45 minutes
Cooking time: 40 minutes, plus cooling

200g (7oz) fresh strawberries, hulled
and halved
200g (7oz) caster sugar
150g (5oz) unsalted butter, softened
3 medium eggs
200g (7oz) self-raising flour, sifted
½ tsp bicarbonate of soda
50ml (2fl oz) buttermilk

For the icing
125g (4oz) unsalted butter, softened
250g (9oz) icing sugar, sifted
green food colouring
ladybird, bumble bee and butterfly sugar
decorations (optional)

1 Preheat the oven to 190°C (170°C fan oven), mark 5. Line a 12-hole muffin tin with paper muffin cases.
2 Put the strawberries and 50g (2oz) caster sugar into a heatproof bowl and cover with clingfilm. Put over a pan of barely simmering water and cook gently for 30 minutes.
3 Meanwhile, using a handheld electric whisk, whisk the butter and remaining caster sugar in a bowl, or beat with a wooden spoon, until pale and creamy. Gradually whisk in the eggs until just combined. Using a metal spoon, fold in the flour, bicarbonate of soda and buttermilk until combined. Divide the mixture equally among the paper cases.
4 Bake for 20 minutes or until golden and risen. Leave to cool in the tin for 5 minutes. Meanwhile, pass the strawberries and juice through a sieve into a shallow bowl. Discard the strawberries.
5 Using a cocktail stick, prick the top of the cakes all over. Dip the top of each cake into the strawberry syrup, then transfer to a wire rack to cool completely.
6 For the topping, put the butter into a bowl and whisk until fluffy. Gradually whisk in half the icing sugar, then add 1 tbsp boiling water, a little green food colouring and the remaining icing sugar and whisk until light and fluffy.
7 Insert a star nozzle into a piping bag, then fill the bag with the buttercream and pipe in a zigzag pattern on top of each cake. Decorate with the sugar ladybirds, butterflies and bumble bees, if you like.

Per cupcake
398 cals; 20g fat (of which 13g saturates);
53g carbohydrate; 0.5g salt

Sea Breeze Cupcakes

makes 12

Preparation: 40 minutes
Cooking time: 20 minutes, plus cooling

1 pink grapefruit (about 350g/12oz)
50g (2oz) ready to eat dried cranberries
250g (9oz) self-raising flour, sifted
125g (4oz) caster sugar
50ml (2fl oz) milk
1 medium egg, beaten
75g (3oz) unsalted butter, melted
1 tsp baking powder

For the icing and decoration
300g (11oz) fondant icing sugar, sifted
red and yellow food colouring
50g (2oz) apricot jam
edible silver balls
cocktail umbrellas (optional)

1 Preheat the oven to 190°C (170°C fan oven), mark 5. Line a 12-hole muffin tin with paper muffin cases.

2 Grate the zest from half the grapefruit into a bowl. Set aside. Cut the top and bottom off the grapefruit and stand it upright on a board. Using a serrated knife, cut away the pith in a downward motion. Cut in between the membranes to remove the segments. Whiz the segments in a food processor until puréed.

3 Transfer the purée into the bowl with the zest. Add the cranberries, flour, caster sugar, milk, egg, melted butter and baking powder and stir with a spatula until just combined. Divide the mixture equally among the paper cases.

4 Bake for 20 minutes or until golden and risen. Leave to cool in the tin for 5 minutes, then transfer to a wire rack to cool completely.

5 For the icing, put the icing sugar into a bowl and add enough water (2–4 tbsp) to make a smooth icing. Add a few drops of food colouring to make it pinky-orange in colour. Brush the tops of the cakes with the apricot glaze, then spoon a little icing on to each cake to flood the top. Decorate with the silver balls. Stand the cakes upright on the wire rack and leave for about 1 hour to set. Decorate with a cocktail umbrella once set, if you like.

Per cupcake
287 cals; 6g fat (of which 4g saturates);
61g carbohydrate; 0.1g salt

Truffle Kisses Cupcakes

makes 18

Preparation: 40 minutes
Cooking time: 30 minutes, plus cooling and setting

150g (5oz) unsalted butter, softened
200g (7oz) caster sugar
3 medium eggs
75g (3oz) self-raising flour, sifted
200g (7oz) plain flour, sifted
½ tsp bicarbonate of soda
75g (3oz) roasted chopped hazelnuts
200ml (7fl oz) buttermilk
15g (½ oz) plain chocolate, finely grated

For the topping and decoration
200ml (7fl oz) double cream
150g (5oz) plain chocolate
100g (3½oz) milk chocolate, finely chopped
18 small chocolate truffles (optional)

1 Preheat the oven to 180°C (160°C fan oven), mark 4. Line a 12-hole and a 6-hole muffin tin with paper muffin cases.
2 Using a hand-held electric whisk, whisk the butter and sugar in a bowl, or beat with a wooden spoon, until pale and creamy. Gradually whisk in the eggs until just combined. Using a metal spoon, fold in both flours, the bicarbonate of soda, hazelnuts, buttermilk and grated chocolate until combined. Divide the mixture equally among the paper cases.
3 Bake for 20–25 minutes until golden and risen. Leave to cool in the tin for 5 minutes, then transfer to a wire rack to cool completely.
4 For the topping, heat the cream in a small pan until nearly boiling. Finely chop 100g (3½oz) plain chocolate and put into a bowl along with all the milk chocolate. Pour the hot cream over the chocolate and leave to stand for 5 minutes, then stir gently until smooth. Chill the mixture for 15–20 minutes until thickened slightly.
5 Using a palette knife, spread a little chocolate cream over the top of each cake. Finely grate the remaining plain chocolate over the top of each cake. Finish each with a chocolate truffle, if you like. Stand the cakes upright on the wire rack and leave for about 1 hour to set.

Per cupcake
317 cals; 20g fat (of which 10g saturates);
34g carbohydrate; 0.2g salt

Wedding Cupcakes

makes 12

Preparation: 30 minutes

Cooking time: 15 minutes, plus cooling and setting

1 × quantity cupcake mixture (see page 36)

12 pink cupcake cases

pink food colouring paste

500g (1lb 2oz) buttercream (see page 48)

12 rose-themed cupcake surrounds

tip

As the cupcakes are already in single-sized portions it is easy to calculate how many you will need for a wedding party. You can tint the icing to the colour of the theme and buy cardboard cupcake surrounds from specialist cake shops or via websites.

hint

For added wow-factor, roll out coloured sugarpaste (ideally mixed with gum tragacanth – see page 75) until 5mm (¼ inch) thick, then stamp out small heart shapes. You could even pipe the initials of the bride and groom on to the hearts. Stick the hearts (standing upright) into the top edge of each iced cupcake.

1 Make the cupcakes in the paper cases as per the method described. Leave to cool completely before decorating.

2 Dip the tip of a cocktail stick into the desired shade of pink food colouring, then dip the coloured end into the buttercream. Use a spatula to start mixing in the colour, stopping when the buttercream is marbled.

3 Fit a piping bag with a 1cm (½ inch) open-star nozzle and fill with the buttercream. Hold the piping bag just above the centre of a cupcake and start piping with even pressure. Swirl the icing in a spiral from the centre towards the edges, making sure the entire surface of the cake is covered. By starting in the centre (rather than the outside edge as is normal) you should create a rose effect. Repeat with the remaining cupcakes. Leave to set for at least 1 hour.

4 Fit the surrounds around the cupcakes.

Per cupcake

375 cals; 20g fat (of which 12g saturates); 50g carbohydrate; 0.6g salt

Glossary

All-in-one method One of several basic methods for making cakes. Ingredients – usually sugar, eggs, flour and baking powder – are mixed together in a bowl, all in one go.

Almond paste A thick paste made mainly from ground almonds, caster sugar and icing sugar and egg whites. Usually used to cover fruit cakes, it provides a flat surface for icing and adds great flavour. Almond paste is sometimes mistakenly called marzipan, although the latter has less ground almonds and more sugar.

Angelica Crystallised strips of the stems of the angelica herb. Green in colour and used for decorating cakes and desserts.

Baking parchment A non-stick baking paper that is used to line cake tins in certain recipes. Also ideal when making chocolate and sugar decorations to ensure nothing sticks.

Baking powder A raising agent consisting of an acid, usually cream of tartar, and an alkali, such as bicarbonate of soda. It is activated when it gets wet and produces carbon dioxide. This expands during baking and makes cakes and breads rise. Some baking powders are also heat activated.

Beat To incorporate air into an ingredient or mixture by agitating it vigorously with a spoon, fork, whisk or electric mixer. The technique is also used to soften ingredients.

Bind To mix beaten egg or other liquid into a dry mixture to hold it together.

Blanch To immerse food briefly in fast-boiling water to loosen skins, such as on nuts, or to remove bitterness.

Buttercream A soft icing made by creaming together unsalted butter and icing sugar. Used to cover and fill cakes.

Calorie Strictly a kilocalorie, this is used in dietetics to measure the energy value of foods.

Caramel The stage at which dissolved and heated sugar crystals turn a deep brown.

Caramelise To heat sugar or sugar syrup slowly until it is brown in colour – that is, it forms a caramel.

Caraque Chocolate curls used to decorate cakes.

Chill To cool food in the fridge.

Combine To stir two or more ingredients together until mixed.

Compote Mixture of fresh or dried fruit stewed in sugar syrup. Served hot or cold.

Consistency Term used to describe the texture of a mixture – for example, firm, dropping or soft. The consistency of piping icing is very important for the piping to be a success.

Coulis A smooth fruit purée, thinned if necessary to a pouring consistency.

Couverture Chocolate with a relatively high proportion of cocoa butter. Used mainly for confectionery, as it dries to a hard, shiny finish. Needs to be tempered before using (see Temper).

Cream (ingredient) Made from the butterfat layer skimmed off the top of milk. Different types contain different percentages of butterfat, the higher the percentage, the easier the cream is to whip. Single cream (18% fat) has the thinnest consistency. It is not suitable for whipping and is used for pouring and in cooking. Whipping cream (at least 38% fat) can be whipped to twice its original volume. Double cream (48% fat) can be poured or whipped. Extra-thick cream is single or double cream that has been homogenised to give it a thicker consistency, generally used only for spooning. Clotted cream (55% fat) does not need to be whipped and is generally not used during cooking since it separates when heated. Soured cream (18% fat) is single cream treated with a bacteria culture to give it a slightly sour taste and a thick texture. Crème fraîche (39% fat) is similar to soured cream, but slightly milder and softer. Creams with a fat content of 35% or above are suitable for freezing for up to two months.

Cream (technique) To beat together fat and sugar either by hand or using an electric mixer until the mixture is pale and fluffy. This method is frequently used in cake making to incorporate air.

Cream of tartar Also known as tartaric acid, this is a raising agent that is also an ingredient of baking powder and self-raising flour.

Crème pâtissière A rich egg custard that is often used to fill cakes and pastries, such as profiteroles and éclairs.

Crimp To decorate the edge of a pie, tart, shortbread or cake by pinching it at regular intervals to give a fluted effect. Special crimping tools are used to give a decorative edge to fondant-iced cakes.

Crystallise A preserving technique mainly applied to edible flowers, petals, herbs, leaves and small fruit.

Curdle When the solid and liquid components of a mixture separate. In cake making, this usually happens when the egg is added too quickly to the creamed mixture. A curdled cake mixture will result in a heavy cake.

Dowel Inserted into sugarpasted cakes to support the tiers. Usually acrylic, they are hygienic and, once in place, trimmed to the desired level.

Dredge To sprinkle food generously with flour, sugar, icing sugar, and so on.

Dropping consistency Term used to describe the required texture of a cake or pudding mixture just before cooking. Test for it by taking a spoonful of the mixture and holding the spoon on its side above the bowl. The mixture should fall of its own accord (but reluctantly) within 5 seconds.

Dust To sprinkle lightly with flour, cornflour, icing sugar, and so on.

Edible glue Widely available from all specialist cake shops or via websites, edible glue is suitable for all sugarcraft purposes – especially in figure modelling and flower making.

Extract A concentrated flavouring, such as vanilla or almond. Extracts should be used in small quantities.

Feather ice Decorating technique that involves dragging a skewer through two contrasting-coloured icings.

Flour Generally made from grinding wheat, this is the basis for breads, cakes and pasta, among other basic recipes. White or plain flour has had most of the wheat germ removed and is commonly used in cakes, in conjunction with a raising agent such as baking powder, as well as in biscuits, pastry and some breads. Self-raising flour is plain flour with a raising agent included. Wholemeal flour contains the whole of the wheatgerm, producing a denser result, which is higher in fibre. Strong flour is made from high-gluten wheat varieties, which helps dough to expand and rise. It is often used for bread making. Gluten-free flour is usually made from a combination of ground rice, potato, buckwheat and maize.

Flower paste Modelling material that's ideal for making intricate, ultra-fine decorations like flowers, leaves, bows and frills, as well as intricate plaques to rest on cakes. It is easy to use and dries very hard without being too brittle.

Folding in Method of combining a whisked or creamed mixture with other ingredients with limited air being lost. Use a large metal spoon (which will cut cleanly through the mixture): keep scooping down to the bottom of the bowl, then turning the mixture on top of itself, while at the same time giving the bowl a quarter twist. Continue folding in this fashion just until the ingredients are combined – do not be tempted to over-fold the cake mixture or it will lose air, resulting in a heavy cake.

Fondant icing See Sugarpaste.

Food colour Available in liquid, paste or powder form. Add minute amounts with the tip of a cocktail stick until the desired colour is achieved.

Frosting A type of cake icing, often used warm, which is generally light and fluffy.

Ganache A rich filling or coating for cakes, choux buns and biscuits, made from chocolate and double cream.

Gelatine An animal-derived gelling agent, sold in both powdered and leaf forms. Vegetarian alternatives are available.

Glaze A glossy coating given to sweet and savoury dishes to improve their appearance and sometimes flavour. In cake decorating, apricot glaze is the most common.

Grate To reduce a solid food (such as citrus zests or chocolate) to coarse or fine threads by repeatedly rubbing it over the surface of a grater.

Greaseproof paper An all-purpose non-stick baking paper suitable for lining cake tins. Once the tin is lined, grease the paper lightly.

Grind To reduce foods such as coffee beans, nuts and whole spices to small particles using a food mill, pestle and mortar, electric grinder or food processor.

Gum arabic Also known as acacia gum, this is a powder that can be used to make an edible glaze, adhesive or thickener.

Gum tragacanth A natural gum that strengthens many types of icing. Just a little of it kneaded into sugarpaste (follow directions on the pot) will make the sugarpaste easier to handle and cause it to dry harder. A worthwhile investment.

Hull To remove the stalk and calyx from soft fruits, such as strawberries

Infuse To immerse flavourings, such as spices and vanilla, in a liquid to impart flavour. Usually the infused liquid is brought to the boil, then left to stand for a while.

Knead To work dough by pummelling with the heel of the hand. Sugarpaste and cocoform often need to be kneaded prior to use to make them softer.

Macerate To soften and flavour raw or dried foods by soaking in a liquid – for example, soaking fruit in alcohol.

Marble When two contrasting mixtures are not completely combined.

Mocha A term that has come to mean a blend of chocolate and coffee.

Muffin case Disposable paper cases used in a bun or muffin tin for baking cupcakes and muffins

Muffin tin Tray of cup-shaped moulds for cooking small cakes and deep tartlets. Also called a bun tin.

Pare To finely peel the skin or zest from fruit. There are paring tools to help get even strands of skin or zest.

Patty tin Tray of cup-shaped moulds for cooking small cakes and deep tartlets. Also called a bun tin.

Pestle and mortar Marble, wood or porcelain bowl with a heavy grinding tool for grinding herbs, spices, nuts, and so on.

Pipe To press a soft substance such as icing or cream through a piping bag, which may or may not be fitted with a piping nozzle.

Pith The bitter white skin under the thin zest of citrus fruit. Try to avoid putting this into recipes that call for the zest of citrus fruits, as it is bitter.

Plaque A rolled-out piece of sugarpaste that is cut to size and left to dry before being mounted on a cake (usually with a message written on it). Plaque cutters of varying shapes and sizes are sold in specialist cake shops or via websites.

Plunge cutter Cutters that eject the sugarpaste shape by use of a spring plunger. They are wonderfully easy to use and come in a huge variety of designs.

Praline A combination of nuts (usually almonds) and caramel that is left to dry and then crushed to a powder. Often used to decorate the sides of cakes.

Purée To pound, sieve or liquidise fruit to a smooth pulp. Purées often form the basis for sauces.

Reduce To fast-boil a liquid in an uncovered pan to evaporate water and concentrate the flavour.

Royal icing A traditional white icing made mainly from icing sugar and egg whites, which dries to a hard finish. It is used for covering fruit cakes and also for piping decorations.

Rub-in Method of incorporating fat into flour by rubbing between the fingertips, used when a short texture is required. Used for pastry, cakes, scones and biscuits. This process can be speeded up by pulsing the mixture in a food processor.

Run-out Method of icing biscuits or cupcakes by piping a shape with royal icing and then 'flooding' it with thinned icing.

Run-out film Fine transparent plastic film that can be used for making accurate run-out decorations, which slide easily off the film when they are dry.

Sharp peak A consistency of icing ideal for piping, as it will hold its shape. To test, draw a spoon out of the icing, the icing should form a fine, sharp point.

Sieve To press food through a perforated sieve to obtain a smooth texture.

Sift To shake dry ingredients through a sieve to remove lumps.

Simmer To keep a liquid just below boiling point.

Soft peak A consistency of icing good for spreading over cakes. To test, draw a spoon out of the icing, the icing should form a fine point that just curves over at the end.

Springform tin Also known as a spring-release tin, this is a round cake tin with a spring-release side and removable base, which is clamped in when the spring is tightened.

Straight edge A long, inflexible metal ruler, which is used to obtain a smooth, flat finish on the surface of a royal iced cake.

Sugarpaste Pliable, all-purpose icing made from icing sugar, egg white and glucose, used to cover celebration cakes and for modelling. Gives a rounded, smooth, professional finish. Easy to colour and mould/shape into decorations. Also known as 'fondant' or 'ready-to-roll icing'.

Sugar syrup A concentrated solution of sugar in water used to poach fruit and make sorbets, granitas and fruit juices. Sugar syrup can also be boiled to produce caramel.

Swiss roll tin Shallow, rectangular tin, available in several different sizes, used for baking sponges that are filled and rolled after baking – such as roulades.

Temper A process of heating, cooling and warming chocolate so that it dries with a shine and breaks with a snap.

Torte Rich cake made with little or no flour.

Tepid The term used to describe the temperature at approximately blood heat – 37°C (98.7°F).

Thermometer Used for accurately checking the temperature of boiling sugar syrups

Vanilla sugar Sugar in which a vanilla pod has been stored to impart its flavour.

Whipping (whisking) Beating air rapidly into a mixture with a manual or electric whisk. Whipping usually refers to cream. Whisking can also refer to the basic cake-making technique in which the sugar and eggs are whisked together over a pan of simmering water. Melted butter and flour are then folded into the mixture.

Zest The thin, coloured outer layer of citrus fruit, which can be removed in fine strips with a zester. Avoid using the bitter white pith beneath.

Index

A

afternoon tea carrot cake 101
almond essence 21
almond paste 49–50
  Simnel cake 109
  see also marzipan
almonds: cherry Bakewell cupcakes 152
  pistachio and polenta cupcakes 165
American frosting 47
animals, sugarpaste 77–8
anniversary cake 112
apples, marzipan fruit 86
apricot glaze 49

B

baby bunny Christening cake 114
Bakewell cupcakes 152
baking 24
baking powder 21
baking trays and sheets 15
ballet cake 132
banoffee cupcakes 163
basket weave, piping 60
be mine cupcakes 167
beads, piping 59–60
beetroot: pink cupcakes 160
birds, sugarpaste 77
birthday cakes: Black Forest birthday gateau 102
  chocolate birthday cake 104
  toasted hazelnut meringue birthday cake 113
Black Forest birthday gateau 102
blanching nuts 21
blenders 13
blossom plunger cutter flowers 75
boards *see* cake boards
bowls 14
bows, ribbon 81
brushes 16
butter 21
buttercream 48

covering cakes 42
icing with 55
piping 55
see also frosting; icing

C

cables, piping 60
cake boards 13, 16
  covering with sugarpaste 54
  securing ribbons to 68
cake cutting wires 38
cake separators 71
cake smoothers 16
cake tins 15
  lining 22–3
caramel: banoffee cupcakes 163
  coffee and praline celebration gateau 105
  dry caramel 96
  honeycomb cream cupcakes 162
  praline 96
  problems 97
caraque, chocolate 94
carrot cakes: afternoon tea carrot cake 101
  graduation cake 117
  the ultimate carrot cupcakes 157
carrots, marzipan 86
cherries: Black Forest birthday gateau 102
  cherry Bakewell cupcakes 152
chocolate 89–95
  anniversary cake 112
  Black Forest birthday gateau 102
  chocolate birthday cake 104
  chocolate cake 94
  chocolate cupcakes 151
  chocolate fudge frosting 46
  for coating 92
  decorations 93–5
  dipping 92
  Easter chocolate fudge cake 110
  ganache 48, 107

glacé icing 43
marble cake 35
marbled chocolate cupcakes 154
melting 91
modelling cocoform 95
moulds 92
piping 95
problems 95
red velvet cake 111
Sachertorte 107
tempering 91
truffle kisses cupcakes 170
types of 90
Victoria sandwich 30
white chocolate and orange wedding cake 121
white chocolate cappuccino Mother's Day cake 106
chopping nuts 21
Christening cake, baby bunny 114
Christmas: Christmas tree cake 81
  classic Christmas cake 125
  decorations 79
citrus Victoria sandwich 30
clown cake 131
cocoa 91
cocoform, modelling 95
coconut and lime cupcakes 161
coffee: coffee and praline celebration gateau 105
  coffee fudge frosting 46
  glacé icing 43
  Victoria sandwich 30
  white chocolate cappuccino Mother's Day cake 106
colourings 57
  designing a cake 10
  glacé icing 43
  sugarpaste 54
cookies and cream cupcakes 164
cooling cakes 24
couverture chocolate 90
craft knives 16

cranberries: sea breeze cupcakes 169
creepy-crawly cake 130
crimpers 16
crimping sugarpaste 82
crystallising flowers and leaves 71
cupcakes 36, 147–71
  covering with sugarpaste 67
  filling 67
  flat tops 36
  icing and frosting 67
cups, measuring 14
curls, chocolate 93, 94
cutters 17, 75–6

D

daisies 75, 84
a day at the races 141
decorating 74–79
  modelling sugarpaste 74–9
  with chocolate 92–4
  with sugar 96–7
designing a cake 10
designs: piping 59–62
  run-outs 64
  templates 63
dinosaur cake 136
dots, piping 59–60
dowels 17, 70–1
dried fruit 21
  see also fruit cakes
dropped-thread loop work, piping 60
ducks, sugarpaste 77
dummies, polystyrene 118
dusts, colourings 57

E

Easter: Easter chocolate fudge cake 110
  Easter cupcakes 156
  Simnel cake 109
edible glitter 57
edible glue 75
egg white, crystallising with 87
eggs 21
electrical equipment 13
embossing stamps 16

equipment 13–17
essences 21
extension pieces, sugarpaste 83
extracts 21

F
fairy cakes 36, 150
fat 21
feather icing 66
figures, moulding 85
filling cakes 39
flooding icing 64, 67
florist's wire 16
flour 21
flower paste, modelling 84
flower picks 118
flowers: blossom plunger cutter flowers 75
crystallising 81
fresh flower wedding cake 118
modelling sugarpaste 74–9
piping 65
foam pads 16
fondant icing see sugarpaste
food colourings see colourings
food processors 13
football cake 146
freezing fruit cakes 26
frills, sugarpaste 83
frosting: American frosting 47
chocolate fudge frosting 46
coffee fudge frosting 46
covering a cake with 46
cupcakes 66
filling cakes 39
seven-minute frosting 47
vanilla frosting 46
see also buttercream; icing
fruit: dipping in chocolate 92
marzipan fruit 86
fruit cakes: baby bunny Christening cake 114
calculating quantities 12
classic Christmas cake 125
freezing 26
rich fruit cake 26–7
rosebud wedding cake 122
Simnel cake 109

storing 26, 28
testing 24
traditional mix rich fruit cake 28–9
fudge cake, Easter chocolate 110
fudge frosting 46

G
ganache: chocolate 48, 107
white chocolate 121
gateaux: Black Forest birthday gateau 102
coffee and praline celebration gateau 105
Genoese sponge 32
gingerbread cupcakes 166
glacé icing 43
covering cakes 42
icing with 56
glass cake separators 71
glaze, apricot 49
glitter, edible 57
glue, edible 75
gold leaf 57
golden rules 20
graduation cake 117
grapefruit: sea breeze cupcakes 169
grapes, marzipan 86
graters 16
greaseproof paper 58, 62, 63
green tea cupcakes 159
gum arabic 87
gum tragacanth 73

H
handbag cake 142
hazelnuts: coffee and praline celebration gateau 105
toasted hazelnut meringue birthday cake 113
truffle kisses cupcakes 170
herbs, crystallising 87
honey: lavender and honey cupcakes 158
honeycomb cream cupcakes 162

I
icing: covering cakes 42
cupcakes 66
easy whisked icing 47
feather icing 66

filling cakes 39
flooding icing 64, 67
glacé icing 41, 56
round cakes 53
royal icing 52–3
run-outs 64
square cakes 52
sugarpaste 45
see also buttercream; frosting
icing nails 16
ingredients 21
insertion blades 16
iPod cake 145

J
jugs, measuring 14
jungle cake 139

K
knives 16

L
lace work, piping 62
lattice, piping 60
lavender and honey cupcakes 158
leaves: chocolate 94
crystallising 87
piping 60
sugarpaste 76
lemon: glacé icing 43
marzipan fruit 86
Victoria sandwich 30
limes: coconut and lime cupcakes 161
Victoria sandwich 30
lines, piping 59
lining tins 22–3
liqueur glacé icing 43
liquid colours 57
loaf tins, lining 23
loop work, dropped-thread 60
lustre colours 57

M
Madeira cake 34
marble cake 35
marbled chocolate cupcakes 154
margarine 21
marzipan 50
covering a cake with 51
modelling with 86
Simnel cake 109
mats, sugarpaste 16
measuring equipment 14

melting chocolate 91
meringue birthday cake, toasted hazelnut 113
mice, sugarpaste 77
milk chocolate 90
mini green tea cupcakes 159
mixers 13
mixing bowls 14
mixing spoons 14
mocha glacé icing 43
modelling: cocoform 95
flower paste 84
marzipan 86
sugarpaste 74–9
tools 16
Mother's Day cake, white chocolate cappuccino 106
moulds, chocolate 92

N
nails, icing 17
needles, scribing 16
nozzles, piping 16
nuts 21
coating side of cake with 55
dipping in chocolate 92
praline 97

O
oranges: glacé icing 43
marzipan fruit 86
Victoria sandwich 30
white chocolate and orange wedding cake 121
ovens 24

P
palette knives 14
paper 14
icing bags 58
lining tins 22–3
templates 63
paste colours 57
penguins, sugarpaste 78
pens, food colouring 57
petals, crystallising 87
photographs, edible 83
pillars 16, 70
pineapple, marzipan 86
pink cupcakes 160
piping 56–60
buttercream 55
chocolate decorations 93
designs 59–62
flowers and leaves 65

icing cupcakes 66
problems 66
royal icing 44
techniques 60–2
piping bags 16, 58
piping nozzles 16
piping pumps 16
pistachio and polenta
cupcakes 165
plain chocolate 90
planning 10–11
plastic cake separators 71
polenta: pistachio and
polenta cupcakes 165
pollen dust 57
polystyrene dummies 118
portion chart 25
praline 97
coffee and praline
celebration gateau 105
problems: cakes 37
caramel 96
chocolate 95
piping 66
pumps, piping 16

Q
quantities: fruit cakes 12
royal icing 44
shaped cakes 12
Victoria sandwich cake
12

R
racks, wire 14
raspberry ripple cupcakes
155
red velvet cake 111
ribbon insertion 69
ribbon slotters 16
ribbons 68–9
rich fruit cake 26–7
rolling pins 14, 16
rose water glacé icing 43
roses: Christmas roses 79
modelling sugarpaste
77–8
rosebud wedding cake
122
rosettes: icing cupcakes 60
piping 60
round cakes, royal icing 53
round tins, lining 22
royal icing 52–3
classic Christmas cake
125
flooding icing 64, 67
to marzipan a cake 51

round cakes 53
square cakes 52
tiered cakes 70
rulers 14
run-out film 16
run-outs 44, 65

S
Sachertorte 107
scales 14
scissors 14
scrapers 17
scribing needles 16
scrolls, piping 60
sea breeze cupcakes 169
secret garden cupcakes 168
self-raising flour 21
servings, estimating 25
seven-minute frosting 47
shaped cakes: calculating
quantities 12
lining tins 23
shavings, chocolate 93
shells, piping 60
side scrapers 16
sides, coating with nuts 55
sieves 14
silver leaf 57
Simnel cake 109
Sleeping Beauty's castle 129
smoothers 16
snowman, sugarpaste 79
spatulas 14
spirals, piping 60
splitting cakes 38
sponge cakes: Genoese
sponge 32
Swiss roll 33
testing 24
Victoria sandwich 30
whisked sponge 31
spoons 14
spun sugar 97
square cakes: lining tins 22
royal icing 52
stacked cakes 71
stamens 16
stamps, embossing 16
stencilling, colour dusts 57
sticky gingerbread
cupcakes 166
storing cakes 26, 28, 37
straight edges 16
strawberries: marzipan
fruit 86
secret garden cupcakes
168
white chocolate and

orange wedding cake
121
sugar 21, 96–7
dry caramel 96
praline 96
problems 97
spun sugar 97
sugar thermometers 16
sugarpaste 45
Christmas decorations
79
covering cake boards 54
covering cakes 54
covering cupcakes 67
crimping 82
cut-out extension pieces
83
to marzipan a cake 51
modelling 74–9
modelling tools 16
stacked cakes 71
sugarpaste mats 16
swirls, icing cupcakes 67
Swiss roll 33
lining tins 23

T
tape measures 14
tea: mini green tea
cupcakes 159
techniques 22–4
tempering chocolate 91
templates 60, 66, 76
testing cakes 24
thermometers 16
tiered cakes 17, 70–71
time plan 11
tins see cake tins
toadstool 135
toasted hazelnut meringue
birthday cake 113
toasting nuts 21
toffee: banoffee cupcakes
163
tortes: Sachertorte 107
traditional mix rich fruit
cake 28–9
transporting cakes 70
triangles, chocolate 94
truffle kisses cupcakes 170
Turkish Delight: be mine
cupcakes 167
turntables 16

U
the ultimate carrot
cupcakes 157

V
vanilla essence 21
vanilla frosting 46
vegetable peelers 14
Victoria sandwich 12, 30

W
wafer paper, photographs
83
wafers, chocolate 93
wedding cakes: fresh
flower wedding cake 118
rosebud wedding cake
122
wedding cupcakes 171
white chocolate and
orange wedding cake 121
whisked icing 47
whisked sponge 31
whisks, wire 14
white chocolate 90, 92
white chocolate and
orange wedding cake 121
white chocolate
cappuccino Mother's
Day cake 106
wire, florist's 16
wire racks 14
wires, cake cutting 38
wiring flowers 75
wrestlers, sugarpaste 85
writing, piping 62

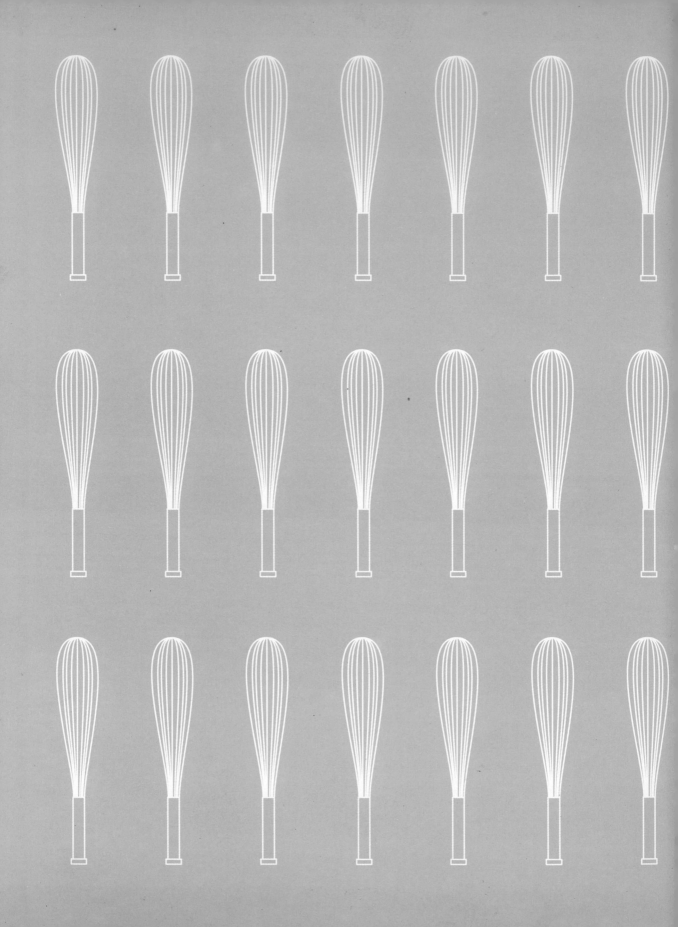